HIGHER THAN THE HILLS

By the same Author

Matthew *(Highland)*

Till the Fat Lady Sings *(Highland)*

About the Author

Bob Jackson was born in Sheffield in 1949 and became a
Government Economic Advisor before being ordained in
1981. He is currently Vicar of St Mary and Holy Apostles,
Scarborough, Yorkshire. He is married to Christine and
they have two surviving children. The story of their eldest
son is told in *Matthew*. For the record, Bob Jackson enjoys
walking, but is less fond of monsoons. He admires Nepal's
people even more than that country's scenery.

For more information about the Church
in Nepal, please contact:
> I.N.F.
> 69 Wentworth Road
> Harborne
> Birmingham
> B17 9SS

> Phone: 0121 4278833
> Fax: 0121 4283604
> Email: ukoffice@inf.org.uk

HIGHER THAN THE HILLS

Bob Jackson

Highland Books

GODALMING
SURREY

First published in 1999 by Highland Books, Two High Pines, Knoll Road, Godalming, Surrey, GU7 2EP.

Cover Photo by the Author

ISBN: 1 897913 48 6

Printed in Finland by W S O Y.

Dedication

To Lok Bahadur Tamang:-

you live the life, I only wrote the story.

Contents

CHAPTER 1

CHILDHOOD'S END

Lok Bahadur Tamang's right arm dramatised every well-remembered detail of the day his childhood ended. As the fist clenched you could smell his fear, as the arm whirled you could see his landslide, as the palm was held to heaven you could hear the desperate cries of his people to their gods.

"It started with a noise like distant thunder. It rumbled from the top of the hill, about a mile high above the steeply sloping village where I was outside playing. I was soaked by the monsoon downpour which had drenched the ground for days. The rain was turning soil to mud, and loosening the grip of the land on the rock beneath. The noise grew louder. I glanced nervously up the stream bed that cut Kapure in two. I was only ten, but I dreaded that ominous noise from the heights above.

"Suddenly, rocks were tumbling down the stream bed in the water. Bigger rocks started crashing down each side of the river. Mud and dust filled the air, and the sky went black. I started choking in the cloud. The roar grew like a jet plane taking off next to me, and the rain pounded remorselessly.

"I ran away to the side of the stream as whole trees started tumbling down the mountain along with the mud and rocks. My father's cattle shed disappeared with the cattle as the land it stood on disintegrated and joined the landslide. Now everyone was running away, but even the land we were running on was crumbling. My whole world was falling to pieces. The outer fabric of the mountain was sliding towards the river below. A great wall of mud crashed down at unimaginable speed with a deafening roar, but I was running and it missed me.

"Then, in horror, I saw my father's land, terraces of millet, maize, potatoes and barley, break its hold on the hillside and disappear below. Now, even if we escaped the immediate danger, my family might starve to death with no land, no crops and no animals to feed us.

"Dodging the trees and rocks hurtling from above, deafened by nature gone berserk, and wide-eyed with terror, I finally made it to the comparative safety of the valley floor. My father, Kom Bahadur Tamang, and my two brothers made it as well.

"As the survivors gathered, everyone was missing relatives and friends. The shock was profound, our fear was hot, our grief was gut-wrenching, and our cries to our gods were desperate. The men confessed their sins and begged the gods to be angry with them no more. They sacrificed chickens to placate the gods, to force them to forgive us and cease the punishment. Using thin bamboo mats, they put up a flimsy shelter from the incessant rain, but I was the only one who got any sleep that night as the others continued to cry to the gods.

"In the morning we counted fifteen bodies, and from the wreckage of their homes, we were able to pull out alive some of the injured. Alas, with no medical help some of these later died of their injuries. After all, we were several days walk from any sort of town up in these hills near the Tibetan border. But if the landslide had come at night instead of in the afternoon we might all have been killed.

"Amazingly, our house had survived the landslide, an untouched island. But, precarious as it was and with no land to farm, it was useless. We had to abandon it, a mocking relic of a childhood that ended that summer's afternoon.

"At last, the rain stopped. We all crossed the landslide for the last time to walk 5 miles to another village to seek sanctuary. As the immensity of the disaster sank in, I had no mother in whose embrace to cry and be comforted. My mother and sister had died the year before. My father had spent what money he had on the local witch doctor—the *Bombo*—hoping his spells and incantations would cure them. But it was money wasted. He wondered if, being poor, he had skimped in the past on the rituals and sacrifices expected. Perhaps the gods had punished him by taking his womenfolk. Now he had lost his house, his land, his cattle, his money, his wife and his daughter. He had become like Job.

"After six months, my father set out for Pokhara to seek work. It's a big town in Western Region. He took my next oldest brother and me with him. The oldest stayed behind, trying to make a living among the big hills of Dhading. At least in Pokhara there would be other Tamang refugees, speaking our tribal language, sharing our culture, and helping us learn the Nepali language and ways.

"But this was 1955, and there were no roads in the whole of Nepal. The walk became a major odyssey. We descended the hill where we took sanctuary and followed a tributary river to the valley of the imposing Anku Khola river. We followed the valley for a couple of days before tackling the hills of Gorkha. Then for days we went westwards, ascending and descending great hills of jungle and rice terraces, following river valleys where possible, always pursued, so it seemed, by the wrath of the mountain gods who had punished us.

"We didn't have a lot of food for the journey, and we drank the water from the mountain streams. We slept under the stars, making flimsy shelters from leaves and branches. It was winter now, so the heat of the afternoon sun was not too intense. But at night we shivered as we huddled together, our teeth chattering in the thin, cold, night air. My brother was sick, but we had to keep moving before the food ran out.

"After many days, the three of us came to a broad and beautiful plateau. At the far end of it was Pokhara, with its paddy fields, its trade and its promise of work. Towering above us, a great snowbound rock rose impossibly high in the north sky, so close we felt we could reach out and touch it. This was the sacred, unclimbed, mountain of Machhapuchhare, the nearest of the Annapurnas to Pokhara. We thought of the summit as the very abode of the glowering gods, looking down with furrowed brows on the doings of men far below, always eager for sacrifices to keep them satisfied, and always ready with their thunderbolts if displeased. But we had made it to Pokhara. From now on the three of us would have to earn money to eat and I would have to grow up fast."

The Tamangs are Buddhists, of a sort, a tribal people originating from Tibet. The village *lama* gave Lok his childhood name—Lung Bahadur. 'Lung' means 'mighty, energetic wind' and 'Bahadur' means 'courage'. This penniless refugee boy would need all his natural energy and courage, not to mention the hurricane breath of the Holy Spirit, if he was to make his mark on the dangerous world that was his inheritance. In fact, this inconsequential boy would soon know the power of the God who is higher than the Himalayas and greater than the mountain spirits. His faith in the God who is higher than the hills was destined to conquer the whole world of fear into which Lung Bahadur Tamang was born.

CHAPTER 2

THE BUND BEATER

Kathmandu, a few days earlier. The *Chowkidar* came back, grinning. He had found me a taxi. The villa was in a quiet part of town, but this morning it was quieter than usual. The car pulled into the courtyard in the pale light of dawn. The taxi driver was prepared to risk it, but he was nervous. He looked round suspiciously as I loaded my rucksack into the boot, but all was peaceful here. The house dog only spoke German. "Guten Morgen, wiedersehen", I whispered into his sleepy ear as I tickled it. I hoped it would be "Wiedersehen" as I had a clear premonition of danger in the trip ahead. Turning to the driver I asked in trepidation, "How much to the airport?"

"Three hundred", came the reply.

"Three hundred?!" I responded.

"There's a *bund*," he explained darkly. I smiled and shrugged my shoulders.

"Okay", I said. I had no choice.

Usually, the main road was chock full of bicycles, motorbikes, auto-rickshaws, tractors, taxis, cars, lorries, minibuses, big buses, cows and humanity. This morning we and the cows had it to ourselves. Even the air was clearer than normal without the daily quota of vehicle and factory fumes getting trapped in the shallow saucer of the Kathmandu valley. I lapsed into momentary poetic reverie:

> There was a green-eyed yellow idol
> to the north of Kathmandu,
> but it choked its way to an early grave
> in the fumes of the traffic queue.

Once upon a time, "The wildest dreams of Kew were the facts of Kathmandu." Now there was little green in the growing city fast drowning in people, vehicles and air pollution.

But my reverie was soon interrupted by a stab of fear. The ancient Toyota, threadbare beyond parody, holes in the floor, no glass in the side windows, shock-absorbers and springs long forgotten, had accelerated down the empty hill as though it were a cliff. I glanced at the speedo but there was none. However, the driver was definitely beating the *bund*. No one could agree whether it was a VAT strike by the traders or a political strike organised by the Maoists against the new emergency powers for the police. But it didn't matter to us one way or the other—a hail of stones was a hail of stones whether it was thrown by shopkeepers or Maoists. I mentally practised lying on the floor around the holes. Back home in Scarborough, where I am Vicar, one of my congregation is a taxi driver: what would Tommy have made of this?

We screeched to a halt at the airport—that was the first time Nepal's answer to Michael Schumacher used his brakes. I stumped up my three hundred and humped my rucksack into the departure lounge. A few days earlier, Royal Nepal Airlines had provided a modern Boeing 757 for my flight from Gatwick. Now it was to be something a little smaller for the domestic flight to Pokhara. There would be eight single seats either side. Problem—the departure lounge was filling with German tourists. Could I beat them to the right hand side of the plane? We had four hundred yards to walk over the tarmac. I beat them in a tight race and settled triumphantly into the front right hand seat just behind the pilot.

For the whole flight to Pokhara this gave me the most stupendous view in all creation: the Himalayas. Towering around and above us through the clouds stood the great white peaks of the Ganesh Himal, the Manaslu Himal, and the Annapurna Himal. The ever changing vista of the most exciting and threatening beauty in the world held every eye except the pilot's in its grip. Fortunately, he kept looking straight ahead. An Indian gentleman, beaten by the Westerners to the left hand side, came over to share my porthole. "Himalayas?" he quizzed, pointing. "No mate, Pennines," I replied in my best Yorkshire. "What's that white stuff?" he persisted. "Icing sugar," I answered, authoritatively. Instantly, I regretted my sense of humour and soon we were talking happily about snow and Manaslu.

All too soon the little plane made a bumpy landing at the airstrip in Pokhara. The length of journey that had taken Lung Bahadur a week or so in 1955 had been accomplished in half an hour. They had built a very nice new terminal building since my last visit. Usually it swarmed with taxi drivers and hotel reps. Today it was abandoned. As we swooped down to land, not a vehicle moved on the roads. The *bund* looked watertight in Pokhara. Strikers and protesters would be at every major junction, stoning anything that moved. I had a full rucksack, a heavy bag and four miles to travel up a hill.

But I was expected, and a hand emerged from the emptiness and waved at me. My friend grinned at me and pointed to a Honda 70, hidden round the back of the building. "Can you ride pillion?" he enquired as if I had a choice. A quarter of a century ago I was the proud owner of a Honda 90. I still regretted selling it to pay for the honeymoon. But I had never ridden pillion in my life and always dreaded the idea. "Of course!" I replied, confidently. The rucksack and bag were a definite problem, so we practised a bit at the airport to get the balance right before setting off for the back streets. At least there was no other traffic to worry about as we picked our way round pot holes, crawling up the hill, keeping a sharp look out for stone throwing gangs.

Pokhara is a large town, well spread out, full of cheaply built two storey concrete buildings but with spaces in between in which to breathe. Down at Lakeside the shops and cafes provide endless fascination and bargains, while the lake is as green and beautiful as they come. Huge hills rise to the south at the far end of the lake, a canoe trip away from town. But they hardly compare with those rising from the northern suburbs. The mountains are as close here as any city in the world. Even Innsbruck does not really compare.

The news was that Lok Bahadur Tamang was trapped by the *bund* down in Nawalparaisi. There were no buses on the roads today. He would have to come tomorrow and we would start the interviews for the book the next day. It was disappointing, but then who could complain at having unexpected leisure time in Pokhara?

Late the next day, Lok finally appeared, straight off an eight hour bus journey. He strode in to meet me, exuding energy, a pleasant smile-filled face, Nepali hat set at a jaunty angle, and bursting with stories to tell. He was 5' 3" tall, 52 years old, with Tibetan features and complexion, thin of limb with strong, small hands, animated and purposeful. Lok Bahadur spoke six languages—his original Tamang, four other tribal languages, and Nepali itself. But his English was no better than my Nepali. Sign language and laughter were all we managed that day. The rest would have to wait for the interpreter in the morning.

Lok Bahadur's life had spanned the whole growth of the Christian Church in Nepal from its very beginning through the incredible development of what may be the fastest growing national church in the world. He told me how he came to lose his childhood home in the high Himalayan hills and arrive as a hungry refugee in Pokhara. It was in this very town that his incredible Christian story began, and now I asked him to tell it to me.

CHAPTER 3

A GOD OF LOVE

"We settled in Ghachok, a shanty town just outside Pokhara. As my father had no land anymore, the only way we could eat was if we found work. My father worked as a porter when he could, carrying on his back the trade route goods out of Pokhara to the foothills of Annapurna and on into Mustang and Tibet. I earned a little from doing odd jobs for other people—looking after goats, protecting rice fields, or being a household servant.

"But the two of us barely earned enough to buy food for three. My brother had been unwell even in Dhading and the journey debilitated him. For two whole years he lay sick at home. We left all but one of the household gods behind in Dhading. The one my father rescued took pride of place in our shanty dwelling. It required a constant supply of rice and other food to keep it happy. Then it would grant us favours and heap no more sorrow on our family. But often we couldn't afford the sacrifices, going hungry ourselves. In the tradition of our people, my father believed that the god was now taking its revenge on his son. My brother would die as surely as my mother and sister. Would there be no end to our tragedies?"

Until 1951, four years before the landslide demolished Kapure, Nepal had been a land closed to foreigners and without a single Christian living in it. However, many ethnic Nepalis lived in India and some of these became Christians, especially in Darjeeling to the east and the border towns to the south. Some of them had prayed for many years for Nepal, the last land of mystery, to be opened up to the Gospel of the God of Love. Some of them waited right on the border, praying for the historic moment to arrive when they could share this good news inside Nepal.

The country was ruled by a family of nobles called the Ranas. They kept Nepal isolated, suppressing all dissent and keeping King Tribhuvan more or less under house arrest in his palace. Then in 1951, he escaped with his family from the palace on the pretext of going for a picnic. He went to the Indian embassy and from there he managed to get away to India. Meanwhile, a well co-ordinated armed revolt was begun and the Ranas were overthrown. The King made a triumphal return to Kathmandu, and the new Government pledged to open up Nepal to the modern world. And so, at last, during the early 1950s these few Nepali Christians were able to enter their homeland and start sharing the Gospel of the God of Love.

The first church in Nepal was founded at Ram Ghat in Pokhara. One of the first Christians to return to his own country was called Noah. One day in 1957, Noah and a friend from the new Ram Ghat church were walking along a footpath leading westwards out of Pokhara, praying for an opening to share the news about the love of Jesus who heals the sick and the broken-hearted. Years later, this footpath was to become the busy Baglung Road, to reek with the smell of diesel, and to echo to the sound of bus and lorry tackling the great hill of Naudanda around its endless hairpin bends. Western tourists in taxis would cast expectant glances to the trail that would carry them upwards to desecrate the Annapurna Sanctuary with their Coca Cola bottles. But, as yet, all this progress was undreamed of by those who walked this quiet footpath.

On the way, Noah and his friend met a weary man, resting his *doko*-load of medicinal herbs under a tree in the heat of the afternoon sun. He had been scouring the jungle up the valley sides for the herbs, which he hoped to sell in Pokhara to feed his sons. His name was Kom Bahadur Tamang.

"It's quite normal in Nepal," explained Lok, "to ask about a stranger's private business, and Noah quickly found out about my father's family situation. I think he may have sensed some goodness in these men, who took the trouble to talk sympathetically with a low caste Tamang like himself. So he risked a fairly desperate request, 'Now my son is sick and I can't afford the treatment. I think he will die just like my wife and daughter. Can you help?'

"Noah gave a surprising reply. 'We can't pay for the treatment—we're as poor as you. But we will come and pray for your son if you like, and we'll ask God to heal him.' My father must have been ready to clutch at any straw, and he arranged to meet the men the next day in Pokhara after he had sold his herbs.

"And so, the next day, the *doko* basket empty, my father led the two strangers to our shack in Ghachok, anxious to find out how we were getting on. The house was made of small bamboo mats in the shape of a nissen hut, and it measured twelve feet by sixteen feet. The sloping roof meant it was only possible to stand up in the very middle. My brother was lying down on a mat on the floor, his body emaciated. He had not been able to eat for some time. There was pain in every part of his body, but his stomach was especially agonising. I was there, doing what I could for him, but feeling helpless inside.

"Noah did not pray with my brother immediately. Instead, he sat us down and explained to us that the one God who had made the whole earth was a God of love. His reaction to human sin was not to punish us in anger but to give us his own Son, Jesus, to be the sacrifice for sin, for all people, for all time. He died so that we could be forgiven without continually making our own sacrifices. And Jesus shows His love for people today by healing their diseases. If we pray in His name, He has the power to heal the sick today because He rose from the dead and is alive today. We can't buy favours from the true God with money, but we can ask for them through prayer, and He gives freely, simply because He loves us.

"Then Noah laid his hands on my sick brother and prayed to Jesus that he be made well again. As he prayed, the terrible pains all left his body, never to return. When Noah had finished, my brother was able to sit up and eat a thin soup made from maize flour. Over the next few days he continued eating and getting stronger until he was completely fit and well. A few years later he became a Gurkha soldier in the Indian Army."

The moment when his son ate the soup was the pivotal moment of Kom Bahadur Tamang's life, when hope conquered the rising tide of despair. He realised that the love of Jesus could overturn the fear of the old gods, and he threw out his remaining household idol. It would have no more power over him.

"I decided," added Lok, "that I would believe in Jesus from now on as well, because I had proof of His reality and of His love. He was higher and greater than any mountain God. Pastor David Mukhia, the first Christian pastor in Nepal, baptised my father and later I too, was baptised.

"My brother also believed for a while. But, after he joined the army and married a *lama*'s daughter, he reverted to the old religion. But for my father and I, there was to be no turning back. It was the God of love for us from now on."

CHAPTER 4

STARTING A NEW LIFE

"Ram Ghat church was too far away in Pokhara to get to every week. Instead, a small fellowship formed in Ghachok, and a group of us made the trip to Ram Ghat every two or three months. It was in Ghachok that I first came across opposition. The township was in two parts—upper Ghachok was inhabited by the Gurung tribe, and Lower Ghachok by caste Hindus, some lower caste and some Brahmins. We tried hard to share the Good News in both places, but we made very little impression. The only converts came from the people who lived on the edges of the village, and even they were forced to flee their homes when it became known they were Christians. They all went to live in Pokhara where they could be anonymous in the town."

Lung began to feel about Ghachok how Jesus felt about Capernaum—being given every opportunity to repent and believe but refusing to do so. Like Jesus, he would need to go elsewhere with his evangelistic zeal. As Lung grew up, he managed to learn to read and write in Nepali even though he was never able to attend a school. He also grew as a Christian, though again with little formal training.

"My best opportunity came in 1963 when I attended a two week Bible School run by Robert Karthak, one of the founding fathers of the church in Nepal. New songs were being written, and one of them became a favourite of mine:

> Open the door, open the door
> Why don't you open the door?
> The Lord's come for you, to give
> You the gift of Salvation!

"This 'gift' of salvation was a wonderful thing to a boy whose old gods demanded high payment for small favours. So I opened the door of my heart and let him in. By 1965 I was grown up and already one of the leaders of the small fellowship in Ghachok. It was the centre of my life.

"I also registered my citizenship, for which I needed a Nepali name. They thought 'Lung' was a barbaric Tamang name, so I had to pick a new one. 'Lok' sounded as close as I could get in Nepali, and it had a neutral sort of meaning—'man' or 'people'."

And so Lung Bahadur became Lok Bahadur as Abram had become Abraham when God promised he would be the father of a great people. Lok in his turn was to be the spiritual father of many people. But to do so he would need to live up to the literal meaning of his new name—'Man of Courage'

Although most of Nepal is composed of giant hills leading up to Himalayan peaks, there is a thin strip of flat land in the south known as the Terai. Geographically, the

Terai is the very northern edge of the great North Indian Plain, but it was filled with impenetrable jungle in which tigers roamed and malaria ruled. Now, however, the jungle was being cut back and malaria being defeated. This flat land was becoming habitable and productive. It was Nepal's frontier land—a safety valve for the growing population of the hills that hill farming couldn't feed. The Government was allocating much of the Terai land in a scheme called *Sukum Basi*—'Land for the landless'.

"I heard about *Sukum Basi* and it seemed it was for people like me, so I decided to investigate it. One morning I set out with a friend to find the area of Nawalparaisi where the land was being given and see if we could have some of it. It might even be flat! It was a nice, sunny morning as we set off, but, after a while, we noticed that a small bite seemed to have been taken out of the sun. Then more of it disappeared. The daylight began to drift away, and soon it became pitch dark. The cattle in the nearby fields and sheds all cried out in alarm, and my friend panicked. He decided it wasn't an auspicious day on which to embark on this quest! So back home we went as the sun began to reappear from behind the moon and the eclipse finished.

"The next day we set out again. We carried our food with us, mainly maize flour, together with pots and pans for cooking by a river in the evenings. Then we would sleep under the trees as best we could. We couldn't follow a direct line from Pokhara to Nawalparaisi, as there was no bridge over the big river, the Kali Gandaki, in those days."

Having risen in Tibet and cut right through the Himalayas between Annapurna and Dhaulagari in the world's deepest valley, the Kali Gandaki turns eastwards for 50 miles between the hills before spilling out on to the Terai.

So the pair had to walk South West to where they could cross the river before turning east to the *Sukum Basi* land.

"It took a week's walk to find where the land was being allocated. It was a large shelf of gradually sloping but smooth land, a few hundred feet above the Inner Terai of the Chitwan National Park. There was going to be a new village, called 'Barataidi'. We stayed for two days and I decided this was for me. First I had to return to Pokhara, collect all my belongings, say my goodbyes, and return to negotiate my land.

"But how was I going to finance the trip? I walked the 15 miles into Narayanghat, the nearest town, and bought three gallons of salt at 2 rupees per gallon. With my rice and pans added, I had a 15 kilo load to carry back to Pokhara. It was a tough four day walk, but I was able to sell the salt in Pokhara for 20 rupees per gallon and finance the trip! And so it was that my ten years in Pokhara came to an end.

"I was given 2 hectares of land, much of it already cleared of jungle. I built a house out of the local timber—there was plenty of it about. The land seemed productive, and the smallholding went pretty well. Later, my father came to join me. It felt wonderful to him to have land again after ten years with none.

"I had land in Barataidi but I was lonely. I discovered there were no other Christians in the area at all. In fact, I don't think there was a single other Christian in the whole of Nawalparaisi Region. The Tamangs in Dhading were Buddhists, but down here on the Terai all the people were Hindus. I wouldn't drink or smoke, and this made my social life limited. In Acts chapter 15, the Apostles forbid eating meat that has been offered to idols, and most of the meat in

Barataidi was first being offered to the idols. So it was impossible for me to go to special events or parties and I grew quite skilful at making excuses to stay away! For eighteen months I mourned for my church and friends and fellowship in Pokhara. I was an isolated Christian, in lonely exile, in an alien world.

"At the end of the eighteen months, desperate to end my isolation, but holding on to my faith, I started praying that one of the church leaders from Pokhara, my friend Dhanraj Tamang, would come to see me. Dhanraj had been a Tamang *Bombo*, or witch-doctor, until he became a Christian. Now he was a school storekeeper. But, what I didn't know was that he was recovering from a serious fall and was immobilised for months. I prayed and prayed for more than a year, but no one came to see me. What had happened to the God who seemed so alive and powerful in Pokhara ? I felt abandoned.

"As he was slowly recovering, Dhanraj spent a lot of time in prayer. Suddenly one day, while he was praying, he saw a vision. In his vision, he saw an area covered with large and dangerous thorns, and another area of impenetrable jungle. And God said to him, 'Clear this!' Then God gave him three packets of wheat seed and told him to go first to the East and then to the South. Three times, the same vision came to him, exact in every detail, but even so Dhanraj had no idea what it meant.

"Then, as Dhanraj was getting back on his feet, three Tamangs from Dhading District arrived in Pokhara, looking for him. They were the very first Christians in the area, and they had no church and no pastor. But they did know of Dhanraj. "Will you come back to Dhading with us and baptise us when we get there? We know it will be dangerous to be Christians, and many Buddhists might persecute us, but we're determined.

"Dhanraj began to understand his vision. Dhading was due east of Pokhara, and the three Christians would need to watch out for the dangerous thorns of persecution. So he went back to Dhading along the route we had taken years before, and baptised the three."

One day these hills would ring to the sound of "Jaimese" ("Hail to the Messiah") at every casual meeting, but, as yet, the voices of these three would not be loudly heard in fabled Jharlang. There were many thorns yet to be cleared away.

"Dhanraj now knew he had to go South, but where-abouts? Then he remembered me. He knew I had gone south to Nawalparaisi, and he came looking for me. It took him a while to search me out, but eventually he turned up on my doorstep. It was eighteen months since I had begun secretly to pray for Dhanraj to come, and three years since I'd moved. It was a very exciting day, especially when Dhanraj told me about his vision. After all, I was growing wheat on land cleared from the jungle and so the vision seemed to be for me. Surely now was God's time at last to begin clearing this Hindu jungle and planting the good seed of a Christian church in Barataidi.

"Dhanraj stayed for a week. I invited anyone from the area who was sick to come to my house where Dhanraj and I prayed for them. To my delight, many of them were healed. I'm no doctor so I don't know what they were healed from. I just know they looked really ill, but after we prayed for them, they were better! They were carried in and walked out.

"While some were being healed of ordinary physical ailments, others had perhaps been oppressed by household gods or demons, and their fears had made them ill. Now they were released from their fear into a new faith in the God of love."

The Greek word *'sodzo'* used in the New Testament means both 'to save' and 'to heal'. The act of healing the villagers from their illnesses seemed the same act as that of saving them from the stranglehold of their old religion and superstitions, releasing them into a Christian faith. Prayer conquered illness and faith conquered fear.

"So the jungle was beginning to be cleared, and soon after Dhanraj left, I was able to baptise twenty-five new Christians. Now I had taken the plunge and become a pastor of a Christian church. I was no longer alone."

CHAPTER 5

PICK ANY ONE

But there was another sense in which Lok was still alone. He was twenty-three. He had built his house, and his farm was succeeding. He was hard-working and vigorous. He didn't drink or smoke. He was considerate of others, already developing a pastor's touch. He was cheerful, good fun to be with, and good-looking.

It became a fact universally acknowledged by the fathers of many local daughters that a young man in possession of such fortune must be in want of a wife.

"I was surprised and flattered by the number of high caste Brahmins who called to offer their daughters to me in marriage. Me, a mere low caste country bumpkin tribal from the hills! I thought about this, but decided it was hopeless—none of these girls were Christians, and it was unfair to expect a Brahmin girl to fit into Tamang society. I had to resist the pressure from the neighbours to arrange a local marriage, but I still wanted to get married.

"One day, I was reading the story in Genesis chapter 24 of how Abraham found a wife for his son Isaac. He sent a servant back to his homeland to find a suitable girl, and the servant returned with Rebekah, the daughter of Abraham's brother Nahor. 'That's it!' I thought. There is a tradition of marrying cousins among the Tamangs, and I had several uncles still working the land on the steep hills of Dhading.

"So I resolved on a quest to Dhading to find a wife. First, though, there was a problem. I had to save up enough money to get me there. It took a while to save up eighty rupees, but eventually I was ready to set out on my pilgrimage home for a wife. There were still no roads and no bridge over the Khali Gandaki, so I had to start with the usual westwards diversion before tracking north eastwards on the long trail for Dhading. After many days I began to see old familiar landmarks as I walked up the valley of the Anku Khola. At last, following a bend in the valley, there in front of me was our hill, and my old village of Kapure, now rebuilt as the landslide began to heal. It was the first time I had seen it since leaving that fateful day in 1955.

"I wondered if anyone would remember me, the small boy who had left with his father after the landslide thirteen years ago. I needn't have worried because they didn't just remember me, they were all cross with me. They'd found out I'd become a Christian. So I was met with hostility not indifference. 'What have you been doing taking up this white man's religion? Those missionaries eat with leprosy patients. How do we know you haven't picked up leprosy from them?'

"I liked the hostility because all the questions gave me plenty of opportunities to explain my faith. I told them about my brother and Noah, and about Dhanraj and the healings. I think, as they discovered I was friendly and sincere, some of them even softened towards me.

"Then one day I met a young cousin who I really liked. I talked it over with my uncle and explained that I had no *tika* mark (the red spot you get after doing *puja* worship) on my forehead, drank no home-made spirits, could offer no presents, and would not follow the Tamang religion. Instead, I followed Jesus. I thought all this might put the uncle off.

"'Take her, take her, take her!' he bellowed, full of enthusiasm. 'Just give me a cloth hat and a shawl for my wife.' This seemed a reasonable price, and so I went off to a nearby village, where there was a shop, to buy the hat and shawl.

"As I got near the shop, I bumped into another uncle, who started on the usual tack. 'What are you doing taking up this white man's religion and being a traitor to your people?' So I told the story again, and witnessed to my faith for about an hour. At the end of the hour, my uncle stroked his chin and said, 'Hmm, so you've come here looking for a wife. I've got four daughters, pick any one you like! Have a look at them in turn and choose which one you prefer!!' I explained that I'd already arranged to marry the daughter of the other uncle, and I had only come here to buy the presents at the shop. 'Have you settled it yet? Have you paid for the presents?' he pressed. 'Well, no, not yet, I'm just about to' I replied. 'Then come and see my daughters.' 'No, I can't, I've promised the others.' 'Nonsense, it's not settled yet, just come and have a look.' 'No, I really can't.' 'Oh yes, you can.' This went on for a long time and he wouldn't back down. So eventually I capitulated and was taken on the inspection tour.

"The first daughter was making the local fire-water and didn't seem very friendly. I wasn't impressed at all. Then we found the second daughter. She was making the *rakshi* as well, and she was just as unfriendly. Two down and two to go. We found the third daughter grinding maize. I kept trying to make polite conversation, but all I got in reply were grunts and monosyllables.

"I thought I might as well go to the shop, but my uncle took me by the arm and guided me into the kitchen. The fourth daughter was making a sort of popcorn out of maize over the fire. As soon as I came into the room, she stopped what she was doing, cleared up, gave me a seat and offered me some food. She chatted, all relaxed and friendly, and really looked after me. I was seriously impressed, even smitten. She had a ready smile and laughed at the same things as me. She seemed vigorous and hard-working and wonderfully hospitable. 'This is the one!' I thought to myself, getting all excited. 'This is my Rebekah, the one the Lord is giving me.'

"We talked for about four hours. Her name was Phulmaya and I loved the potatoes she cooked for me. Eventually, my uncle drew me aside. 'I really like her,' I said, 'but I don't wear the *tika*, I don't drink the fire-water, I'm not offering presents, and I don't follow the Tamang religion. I follow Jesus.' 'That's okay, I've been to India and I know there are lots of Indian Christians. It's not just a white man's religion,' replied my uncle. 'You can take her.'"

I wondered what Phulmaya must have been thinking about all this. It didn't seem as though either Lok or her father had asked her opinion before they agreed the deal. A few days later, at home in Barataidi, I was able to ask her side of the story.

"Yes, I was getting a bit anxious. Then my father came to me and said, 'He's one of us, a relative, and he's a good man so you don't have to worry. But it's hot down on the

Terai, and if you can't settle, come back home and I'll give you some of my land and you can always settle down here.' This sounded quite reassuring, but I'd never seen Lok Bahadur before and had no idea what sort of place he was taking me to. I felt scared, but I respected my father so much that when he said, 'Are you happy to go with this man?' I replied, 'Yes, if you say it's the right thing.'"

This left Lok with just two problems. "I had almost run out of money and I suddenly realised I didn't have enough to get two of us back to Barataidi. How could I explain that to Phulmaya? I was lucky. 'That's all right' she said, 'I've got 300 rupees, that should get us there.'

"The other problem was the first uncle. It was just too embarrassing to face him. Next morning, we slipped away for Barataidi by a different route, before he found out and his wrath caught up with me. A year later, I returned to Dhading and called on them with the cloth hat and the shawl, some food, and some very profuse apologies!"

And so Lok and Phulmaya happily set up home together in Barataidi. They grew closer to each other, but there was still one barrier between them. Phulmaya was not a Christian and knew little about Christian things. But this was about to change.

"After two years I became ill with a severe stomach complaint. Lok and his new church prayed for me and, straight after the prayers, I got better. Now I had experience of the love and reality of the God who answered prayer and healed and saved."

So Phulmaya, too, put her trust in the healer from Galilee, and the team that would together face the many trials of Christian ministry in a hostile culture was finally formed.

CHAPTER 6

DEFEAT AND EXILE?

Nepal is the world's only officially Hindu state. When the church in Barataidi began, it was illegal to change religion or persuade someone else to change. The main danger point was baptism because this was the obvious public sign of a new religion. If the convert was reported to the police he could expect a year in gaol. The pastor doing the baptism got six years. This law was only repealed in 1990 after a revolution which overthrew the *panchayat* system through which the king ruled as well as reigned. It was replaced by a parliamentary democracy and constitutional monarchy. After the revolution, Christians still faced unofficial danger and hostility, but no longer any Government persecution.

At first, Lok's church grew slowly and quietly. It consisted of fourteen families and they managed to stay out of trouble. All this changed in July 1972.

It was monsoon time. The air was unbearably hot and sticky. The rice had been planted and the paddy fields were nicely flooded. Every so often a downpour would give relief from the heat and humidity, but they soon built up again. The rivers would flash flood for an hour or two, then disappear again. It was hard to sleep at night. Mosquitoes and other biting insects filled the air. Footpaths were wet, slippery and hard to negotiate. The poorer farmers were running low on food, and there were still three months to go to the rice harvest. There was little farm work to do, people had time on their hands, and tempers were short. There was darkness in the sky and thunder in the air.

"I had just baptised some new Christians and discovered that someone had reported me to the District Police Office. Usually the police would leave us alone unless they were forced to act by someone registering a complaint. Then we discovered all fourteen families in the church had been reported for changing their religion. I think the Brahmins were behind it. They saw us as a threat to the caste system they were head of. They didn't wait for the police to act. A mob surrounded our house. They made a huge, angry noise and there was a lot of confusion. They burst into the house and ransacked it, taking away all our Christian literature and Bibles. There is a terrible animal fear in being the target of a mob, but I got more used to it over the years.

"Later, the police arrived and ordered me to stop my Christian activities. It was a final warning—next time they would arrest me. The other believers got the same warning—revert to good Hindus, or else!

"Most of the Christians were low-class tribals, Tamangs like me. Now the rest of the village started treating us as 'untouchables'. This made life impossible as we had to avoid contaminating other people by getting close to them. We could only use the village tap when no one else was around. We often had to wait for hours for a chance to get water, usually in the middle of the night.

"So there was pressure from both the police and the village, and some of the Christians gave up. But others stuck it out with us through the monsoon. By the end of September some of the villagers began to feel sorry for us and life became more bearable. Slowly we were accepted back and we had passed our first great test of faith. We learnt that it takes courage and perseverance to conquer opposition. It strengthened us and gave us a new joy in finding we could rely on the Lord when things got difficult."

> Consider it pure joy, my brothers, whenever you face trials of many kinds, because you know that the testing of your faith develops perseverance. Perseverance must finish its work so that you may be mature and complete, not lacking anything.
>
> *James 1:2*

"As we had got through this I decided to go on the attack rather than just lie low. Early in October is Dasai—the greatest festival in the Hindu year. Everyone joins a great feast and sacrifices buffalo, goats and chickens to the gods and idols. Because Christians are forbidden to eat meat offered to idols we couldn't join in the celebrations. We would go hungry again. So I prayed that God would stop the sacrifices. They were splitting the community in two between the Hindus and Christians. If the animals weren't offered to idols we could all eat together.

"I'd got friendly with the biggest landowner in the area. Many of the people were his tenants. So I asked him to put a stop to the sacrifices. I thought he would be cross, but he surprised me by saying, 'I'll do it if the *lama* agrees.' The *lama* was a Buddhist priest, of course, but Buddhism and Hinduism get all mixed up round here, and he was needed for the rituals. His name was Aita Singh Lama. Aita said, 'If the landlord says it's all right, I'm happy to stop the sacrifices.' We had a deal.

"Dasai came and the Hindus prepared the rice wine and the animals for the sacrifice as usual. But nothing could start without the landlord and the *lama*. They had both disappeared. They were both too scared to tell the people what they had agreed to. The people searched their homes but they weren't there. They searched the fields, but they weren't there. They searched the jungle and they found the *lama* and brought him back to the village. But they never did find the landlord. He slipped back well after it was all over.

"Now Aita Singh had to explain to the crowd about the deal to stop the sacrifices, and the crowd got angry and accused him of being a Christian too. There was a great commotion and angry shouting. The buffalo earmarked as the major sacrifice got frightened and panicked. It reared up and then it bolted. Now Aita Singh got angry as well. He saw his dinner running away. So he shouted at the top of his voice that if the people let the buffalo escape he would cut their heads off instead of the buffalo's. So they all calmed down. The buffalo made the mistake of calming down as well, and they easily caught it. So Aita Singh simply killed it without the rituals and offerings, and we had won our victory. All the Christians could join in the feast.

"A few weeks later, though, it was the Tihar Festival—the Festival of Lights. It's called Duvali in India.

Everyone had a day or two off, and the men were drinking and grumbling about how we had spoiled Dasai. The chairman of the *panchayat* (the village committee) held a big meeting. It started at six in the evening, just as it was going dark. One of the men was a strong, confident, forceful character and he accused Aita and me of destroying their religion and culture. He stirred the meeting up into a great lynch mob frenzy against us. He's still alive today, but he lost his land and then all his teeth, so he looks really gummy. He's so ashamed of what happened to him and what he looks like that he can't face meeting people these days.

"The meeting decided on an ultimatum to all the Christians. They rounded us up to hear it. 'If you don't bring us all your Christian literature and Bibles this evening to be destroyed, and then publicly reject your Jesus Christ, we'll beat you up and probably kill you.'

"Phulmaya and I didn't move. As the evening wore on, we watched with sinking hearts as one by one the other Christians returned with their books and Bibles, and shouting out that they rejected Jesus Christ. It all took a long time, and it was 2am before the last one had gone through with it and left for home. We were the only ones left. They usually leave the women alone, so Phulmaya was allowed to go home. Now everything was directed at me. One of the women in the crowd took over. 'He's the ringleader. Strip him naked and tie him up. Keep him there freezing to death until he follows the others!' She started spitting at me, and other women followed her. I was aghast that the other Christians had lost their courage. But I was even more aghast at her and her husband who was backing her up. I thought to myself, 'If you stop the Gospel here then you'll be standing in the way of it spreading from Jerusalem to the ends of the earth. And God is making sure it does spread, so in the end it will be you that is destroyed. You can't stand in the way of God. I wonder what your death will be like?' I was thinking of Judas Iscariot.

"Not everyone in the crowd supported the woman. They were arguing about what to do with me. Some were getting tired and drifting off to bed. Aita Singh Lama said I'd been a good friend to him, and they should think very seriously about tying someone up who could freeze to death. They should sleep on it and tie me up tomorrow if they still wanted to. But the woman and her husband, a really big chap, kept cursing me and stirring up the crowd. It was touch and go. I told them I was going off in the morning to visit my uncle in Pokhara. But by 3am even the thought of me slipping through their fingers couldn't keep them excited and the rest of them went to bed.

"I went home and talked things through with Phulmaya. What should I do? I remembered the verses from Matthew chapter 10 when Jesus sent the twelve apostles out on a preaching tour:

> Be on your guard against men; they will hand you over to the local councils and flog you in their synagogues. But when they arrest you, do not worry about what to say or how to say it. At that time you will be given what to say, for it will not be you speaking, but the Spirit of your Father speaking through you. All men will hate you because of me, but he who stands firm to the end will be saved. When you are persecuted in one place, flee to another.

"So we decided I ought to flee. The trouble was I had no money at all and I would need something to get me to Pokhara. Phulmaya went round all the Christians who had just recanted, begging for money for me, but all she got was 5 rupees. I knew I ought to escape before anyone woke up, and at 4.30am I set out to walk over the hills to Pokhara with 5 rupees in my pocket. I also had some yam with salt and chillies to eat. The walk took me three absolutely exhausting days. It was November so the heat in the day-time wasn't too bad, but the nights were getting long and cold. I didn't get much sleep and spent a lot of time shivering, longing for the first rays of the morning sun.

"Hiding with friends in Pokhara, I felt defeated, angry, bitter and exhausted. All my people had turned against me and deserted Jesus. It was as if Christ himself had been defeated. I felt like Elijah after the battle with the prophets of Baal when Jezebel threatened him. I'd met my Jezebel at the village meeting. Elijah, too, had had to run away, complaining he was the only person left on God's side. God told Elijah he had plenty more people of his own. But it seemed to me I really was the only man left in Barataidi. I was alone, defeated and exiled."

CHAPTER 7

THE VENGEANCE OF GOD

Lok Bahadur was a refugee in Pokhara for the second time in his life. The first time he was fleeing from the wrath of the gods, now it was the wrath of his neighbours. God had stepped in to save him last time, but could he do it again?

"I spent some time reading my Bible, trying to let God speak to me. It was when I read Romans chapter 12 that the words leapt out at me like they were coming directly and personally from God:

> Never be lacking in zeal, but keep your spiritual fervour, serving the Lord. Be joyful in hope, patient in affliction, faithful in prayer. Bless those who persecute you; bless and do not curse. Do not repay anyone evil for evil. Be careful to do what is right in the eyes of everybody. If it is possible, as far as it depends on you, live at peace with everyone. Do not take revenge, my friends, but leave room for God's wrath, for it is written, 'It is mine to avenge; I will repay,' says the Lord. On the contrary: 'If your enemy is hungry, feed him; if he is thirsty, give him something to

drink. In doing this, you will heap burning coals on his head.

"So I learnt I must have joy and hope to conquer the despair I felt, and I must love and care for my enemies, and so win everyone over. It was God's job to deal with my enemies, not mine. They were in greater danger than me. God is more powerful than his enemies.

"After two weeks in Pokhara, I decided I ought to get back home to see what was happening. My friend gave me 300 rupees and some clothes so I would have a more comfortable walk back. I was very anxious about what I would find, and what sort of reception I would get. What I found filled me with awe and astonishment.

"The man who had got the mob going with his call to tie me up and let me freeze outside had got drunk one night. He insulted his wife and stepson very badly indeed. His wife's brother decided to take revenge on her behalf. With a group of relatives, he tied him up and bound him to a post for twenty four hours, exactly what the man had wanted to do to me. Soon after, the big man who was the Jezebel lady's husband took ill. I think he had pulmonary TB. He went downhill fast and people said he was going to die. So I went round to visit them, and his wife and children were all there, crying. There was blood streaming from his nose and mouth. I was shocked and said, 'Oh dear! He looks really ill!' As I said that, he looked up at me and, as he saw me, he just died. It was six months to the day after he attacked us that evening at the Tihar Festival.

"I felt so sorry for them and I was still thinking about Romans Chapter 12, so I did what I could and helped the family with the funeral expenses. His wife, whose fate I had so worried about when she was spitting all over me, responded to the love we showed her. She believed and I was able to baptise her. From the moment her husband died, in April 1973, the persecution we had was halved and the church began to grow. All fourteen Christian families trickled back to the church after they had rejected Jesus, and another five families joined us.

"When Dasai came round again in 1974, a large group were drinking spirits outside our house. They were working themselves up led by a ringleader who was quite a wealthy land owner who bellowed out, 'Everybody has put a *Tika* mark on their forehead today, the very poorest have put on a Tika mark, the King and Queen have put on a *Tika* mark, everyone except these Christians! It's all Lok Bahadur's fault! Let's sort him out once and for all.' They sent for me to come out of my house, but I refused. They sent for me again and I refused again. The third time, twelve of them came to get me and I had no choice. They took me to the courtyard outside the ringleader's house. They stripped me and beat me up badly, while a group of women looked on, cursing me. There were a number of Christians around, but all the men ran away. The women were much braver. They picked up burning firewood and charged at the gang to try and rescue me. They got beaten up as well. In the end, some Hindus pulled the mob off me and helped me back home.

"While they were beating me up, I was thinking of Isaiah 33:1

> Woe to you, O destroyer, you who have not been destroyed! When you stop destroying you will be destroyed.

"The rich ring leader had a grown up son. Exactly six months to the day later the son spat in his face and kicked him during an argument. This is the most serious insult it is possible to make. The man came round and told me what had happened. He was crying and said, 'I can't stay at home after an insult like that from my own son.' I offered to let him stay with us, but he said, 'No thank you, I'll go and stay with our daughter and her family.' What he actually did was run away to India.

"Again, exactly six months later he came back. But now he was very ill. His whole body was blown up. He lasted for fifteen days back in his own home. I went round to see him to offer what friendship I could, and he died while I was there, in my sight.

"The effect on the community was even greater this time, I suppose because the same thing had happened twice and it was hard to shrug off as a coincidence. So we had even more freedom. We could have church services, hold prayer meetings, organise conferences, give out tracts, and generally share our faith. The church began to grow and grow. Some of the women who put curses on me while I was being beaten up became Christians themselves. By now, the growth was not just in Barataidi, we were planting new churches all over the area. After a decade of struggle the time of rapid growth had begun.

"As on the previous occasion, I helped with the funeral, giving the family clothes for the body, and preparing the funeral feast. The man's family were so moved by the love we showed them that they became Christians as well. His land was divided up between his sons, and some of them moved away. So they put pieces of land up for sale.

"We were able to buy the courtyard where I was stripped and beaten, and that's where we built our new church building. Where Christians suffer, that is where God builds his church."

I will build my church, and the powers of
death will not overcome it.

Matthew 16:18

CHAPTER 8

THE BITER BIT

The East-West highway through the Terai was opened during this new time of peace and growth for the church. For the first time rapid travel and communication became possible. It was easy for Lok and others to move around the district, and so for new churches to be planted. It is often said that the Gospel only moved quickly through the Roman Empire because the roads were so good at the time. This new road, one of the first in Nepal, arrived at just the right time for the Gospel to spread along it. It also arrived in just the right place. Lok had lived in his house in Barataidi up on the shelf of land overlooking the Terai for over ten years before the road arrived. When it came, it pushed right up to the northern edge of the flat land opposite Barataidi just a short walk from his house, as though the route had been designed just for him. Long distance bus services began straightaway. After years of near isolation, Lok Bahadur was suddenly free to roam the whole country.

"We had peace and churches were springing up in the area. But it all ended on 3rd September 1977. On the Friday, three leaders from the church in Pokhara arrived at our house and stayed with us until Sunday. One of them was Lal Bahadur and another was Hari Bahadur. All day Saturday and then on Sunday morning we prayed and fasted. Then we walked the 10 kilometres to Dharapani. We were the guests of honour at the foundation-laying ceremony for a new church. Some others came along from Barataidi. There were seventeen of us altogether. When we got there, two or three wooden corner pillars were already up, and other pillars were being prepared. The church was just next to the new road, by the side of a house.

"We started a meeting with the Dharapani Christians, but, as we were singing and praising, a huge crowd of perhaps a 1000 people arrived and surrounded us. They must have got themselves well-organised somewhere and the new road meant they could all walk together. They caught hold of the three leaders from Pokhara, the leader of the Dharapani group, and some others and beat them up badly. Lal Bahadur's arm was never right again after it. The fourteen of us from Barataidi managed to slip into the house and hide in the attic with the cobs of corn. It was three in the afternoon on a hot summer's day, and for two hours we hid, praying, while we sweated all over the corn. I felt like Jesus praying in the Garden of Gethsemane. The noise of the crowd was deafening, and all sorts of things were being shouted. It was very confusing.

"About 5 o'clock we heard a more organised cry from the crowd. 'Where's that pastor from Barataidi? We'll get him and kill him. Where is he?' They were threatening the ones outside, so I came out of the house with the other thirteen and showed myself to the crowd. 'Kill them! Kill them!' shouted the crowd. Even the little children started kicking us and taking up the cry, 'Kill them! Kill them!'

"While we were hiding in the loft, though, an off-duty policeman had heard the huge noise of the crowd and come over to see what was going on. He couldn't do much against a crowd of a 1000 by himself, but he wrote a note and sent it off to the police station 10 kilometres away.

"Not everyone in the crowd wanted to kill us. Attracted by the noise, new people seemed to be arriving all the time. We were surrounded. We were pushed, kicked, hit and spat on. But some of the local believers were even more badly beaten. One old lady had to be carried away in a bad state. Some of the crowd were saying, 'These people are only Tamangs. It's their religion. What have they done wrong?' The head of the village *panchayat* also spoke up for us. But there was a *lama* there, Tok Bahadur Lama, from Lamjung up in the hills. He was a massive man, a freak, incredibly tall. 'Tok' means 'Biter' and he was very aggressive. He shouted, 'You must kill Hari Bahadur and Lok Bahadur! If you chop down the trunk of the tree all the branches die as well!' Soon after, he died of TB, although I don't suppose his alcoholism helped."

"The biter bit!

"At last, after it got dark, six policemen, including two senior officers, arrived on a tractor. The officer in charge recognised Lal Bahadur, who was in a bad way on the ground. He was a friend of Lal's son and used to eat regularly at Lal's house. He took control and saved us. He put us into the *panchayat* office and the police guarded the door as the crowd pressed in around it. He tried to calm the crowd. 'You can't just beat up and kill whoever you want to. The King runs the country, not you. These people should be free to pursue their religion if they want to.' But the crowd shouted back, 'No they shouldn't! We're not letting them go.' He tried for an hour to disperse the crowd, but they wouldn't go. But they managed to keep the crowd from us because the policemen had rifles and the officer-in-charge had a pistol!

"Finally, he said, 'Okay, we'll have to take them to the police station.' He picked out thirty strong men from the crowd and allowed them to escort the seventeen of us, three from Pokhara and fourteen from Barataidi, to the police station. We had to walk the 10 kilometres along the road to the station, and by this stage we were exhausted. We hadn't eaten since Friday because we'd been fasting, we'd been beaten up, and it was late at night. We were so tired, if we stopped walking for a moment we fell asleep where we stood. Hari Bahadur was an ex-leprosy patient and he was in real trouble with his bad feet. He kept falling over time after time. When we stopped or fell over, they hit us with sticks to get us going again.

"By 3am we finally made it to the police station and we were put inside with a police guard. The thirty men were put on the roof to sleep while we slept inside. The man in charge of the station was sympathetic to us because he'd been in charge of Pokhara prison when Hari Bahadur had been inside for being a Christian and he seemed to like him.

"At first light, everybody got up. The thirty on the roof shouted at the police, 'Break the legs of the leaders and jail the lot of them for six years!' But now numbers were more even and the police shouted back, 'Shut up and keep quiet!' It was stalemate. In those days the road had only just been opened and there was hardly any traffic on it. You could wait for hours for a bus. But suddenly a bus came from Narayanghat and, at the same time, another one approached in the opposite direction from Butwal. They both stopped at the police barrier together, where the conductors had to sign their names. The police bundled us all out and put the three Pokhara leaders on the bus to Narayanghat, and the fourteen of us on the bus to Butwal. The three found somewhere to rest and sleep in Narayanghat and got home to Pokhara. We got off at Rajhar, the nearest point to Barataidi, and we were safe."

Then Lok burst out laughing, remembering with glee. "The thirty on the roof had to walk home—there were no more buses for hours. But we got a free ride home!"

The Christians had suffered and been traumatised, but they had survived and even had the last laugh over their tormentors. To comfortable western Christians, suffering and persecution are remote and unwelcome possibilities. But does someone who has actually suffered persecution see it differently?

"When persecution and suffering come, the weak, half-hearted Christians fall away. But the ones who really have a mind for God and want to follow Jesus get stronger. We have long meetings, and we pray on and on into the night. Everyone is together, no one thinks of excuses for missing the prayer meetings. When I wanted to pray all night, I used to go and sit high up in a tree where you really can't fall asleep."

Lok burst out laughing again. "Actually, one night I did fall asleep up a tree and I fell off, but I hit another branch and clung on so I was okay! If your mind is on God then the tiredness, the cold and wet, the hardship and the hunger don't matter. You can endure them if you are going through them for Him. It's what Paul says in 2 Corinthians 12:

The Lord said to me, 'My grace is sufficient for you, for my power is made perfect in weakness.' Therefore I will boast all the more gladly about my weaknesses, so that Christ's power may rest on me. That is why, for Christ's sake, I delight in weaknesses, in insults, in hardships, in persecutions, in difficulties. For when I am weak, then I am strong.

"In the old days when trouble came the believers hid in the jungle and endured hardship. Now they get on a bus to Kathmandu or Pokhara—they're all getting soft! But what really troubles me is to see other believers suffer. There is a sense in which I'm responsible, because the churches in this area all come from me originally. I was the first. So I feel helpless, and there is often very little I can do for them except pray. I keep going back to the Bible passages like the Beatitudes and 1 Peter to remind me that, actually, persecution and suffering are good things in the end, and carry their own reward:

> Blessed are those who are persecuted because of righteousness, for theirs is the kingdom of heaven. Blessed are you when people insult you, persecute you, and falsely say all kinds of evil against you because of me. Rejoice and be glad, because great is your reward in heaven, for in the same way they persecuted the prophets who were before you.
>
> *Matthew 5:11-12*

> Dear friends, do not be surprised at the painful trial you are suffering, as though something strange were happening to you. But rejoice that you participate in the sufferings of Christ, so that you may be overjoyed when his glory is revealed. If you are insulted because of the name of Christ, you are blessed, for the Spirit of glory and of God rests on you. If you suffer, it should not be as a murderer or thief or any other kind of criminal, or even as

a meddler. However, if you suffer as a Christian, do not be ashamed, but praise God that you bear that name.

1 Peter 4:12-16

"So a time of suffering and persecution can also be a time of great joy as well. Christians who have suffered often have a joy that comfortable Christians don't have. Joy can come out of pain and conquer it.

"In some ways, the persecution years were the most productive. People were impressed with the determination of the Christians and wanted to know what it was that meant so much to them that they were ready to die for it. Others were affected by God's power to deal with His enemies. Other enemies responded to the love we showed them in return for their persecution. The Christians prayed and witnessed fervently, it was all a matter of life and death, and the church had no passengers."

At the end of 1977, Lok had much to rejoice in. After his escape from Dharapani, the leadership of NCF (Nepal Church Fellowship) invited him to Kathmandu to tell his story to the National Committee. There were no traditional denominations in Nepal at the time. Almost all the churches belonged to the NCF federation. From that day onwards Lok was invited on to the National Committee, so now he was a national church leader. Locally, many of his opponents had died, others were ruined or had left the area, or had become Christians. The church fellowship in Barataidi had grown to over three hundred believers, and five daughter churches had been started in nearby villages. Through many sufferings and trials, things had come a long way since the day in 1968 that Dhanraj Tamang had finally tracked down a lone and lonely Christian in exile on the Terai.

CHAPTER 9

A LESSON FROM ESTHER

Lok always thought hard about dates, and then started counting on his fingers. It wasn't that his memory was faulty, quite the reverse. Until the Bible translators got to work, Tamang was purely a verbal language and so there was a great tradition of storytelling as a way of passing on the history and tradition of the tribe. Lok's memory for detail was as well-tuned as his storytelling skills. His problem was that he reckoned in Nepali years and months, whereas I wanted to know in the usual international numbers *Anno Domini*! New Year's Day is April 13th, so no year or month coincided with my own and confusion could easily reign unless we were very careful.

"It was December 1978," said Lok, concentrating furiously on his mental arithmetic. "We'd been left alone for over a year but now the Government was organising a new round of persecutions, so we all disappeared into the jungle for three days to celebrate Christmas in secret. But it all came to nothing because the Government got diverted by a political struggle with the opposition democrats. So freedom and growth continued and more churches were planted. By Christmas 1980 we felt really free to celebrate Christmas openly and use it for evangelism.

"We were in Lokahar, a village about 12 kilometres West of Barataidi. There were only five or six households of believers in Lokahar, and the meeting was mainly for evangelism. We had about fifty Christians there, including a choir of about twenty, and we'd gathered a crowd of several hundred, mainly Tamangs and Magars. We had invited them for a Christmas feast and then some music and a word from me. It was 22nd December. We managed to eat a whole buffalo between us, so there must have been five or six hundred altogether. We'd put up a sort of tent made out of thin bamboo mats, and lit the area with paraffin lamps. We finished the meal, and were just starting the meeting at about 7pm. Suddenly, a crowd of about forty men turned up, many of them Gurkhas from the Indian Army home on leave. You could tell by their breath they were drunk on *rakshi*. It's about gin strength. But they were armed and well-organised.

"'Take your foreign religion elsewhere or we'll do you in' was the gist of what they shouted. I thought to myself, 'We've planned this meeting for God, he's going to look after us and make it a success. I'm not afraid, I've got peace about this.' A verse from 2 Chronicles came to mind and I read it out to the people:

As they began to sing and praise, the Lord set ambushes against the men of Amman and Moab and Mount Seir who were invading Judah, and they were defeated. The men of Ammon and Moab rose up against the men of Mount Seir to destroy and annihilate them. After they had finished slaughtering the men from Seir, they helped to destroy one another.

2 Chronicles 20:22,23

"I said to them, 'So all we have to do is to sing and praise, and the Lord will do the rest'. I shouted to the choir, 'Sing hymn 68!' As the choir began singing, 'Jesus the king came down to overcome Satan' the gang began to argue among themselves. As the choir carried on singing, they began pushing each other and fighting among themselves. Some of them started chasing the others. By the time the choir had finished singing, they'd all gone and we were able to carry on with the meeting. The people in the crowd were so taken with the singing and the way the mob turned on each other while the choir sang that they all stayed and listened to us until after midnight.

"Afterwards, we found out that the village *panchayat* in Lokahar had reported me and twenty-eight other church leaders, including all the pastors in our group, to the police station, and then to the Chief District Officer. The District Officer ordered the police to break up the whole church in the area, everything we had built. Most of the leaders scattered and went into hiding, but I stayed on.

"Three weeks later, January 13th 1981, I was leading the church service in Barataidi. I'd never cried in church before, but as I tried to preach, I started to cry uncontrollably for about 10 minutes. Apart from a general sense of foreboding and sadness, I had no idea of the reason. I had a nasty feeling I would soon find out.

"There was only one Christian in the village of Bandipur, 17 kilometres North of Barataidi, through the jungle and up into the hills. He came to church with us when he could, but he'd been a lone Christian in his village for four years. A few days after I'd been crying, he arrived at our house in high excitement. 'Five people have become Christians in Bandipur, won't you come tonight and baptise them?' We had a Bible study fixed that evening at church, so I promised I would come the next day, and he went off back to Bandipur to make preparations.

"That night, I had a nightmare about persecution. In the morning I said to Phulmaya, 'Our persecution is coming, but I don't know where. Maybe it will be in Bandipur. What should I do? If I don't go, five or six believers will be lost. If I do go, we may suffer persecution.' So we prayed about it together and then she said to me, 'Go to Bandipur but take a friend with you. I'll gather some of the women together and we'll pray for you all the time you are away.'"

Lok was a notoriously fast walker, the sort who is only really happy if he sets his own pace. "I hope the other chap was fit," I thought to myself. Lok took up the story again.

"I usually walked alone, but I found my brother-in-law and he walked to Bandipur with me to keep me company. When we got there, I spoke to the people involved, but they seemed lethargic, apathetic, unenthusiastic about baptism and it didn't seem right to go through with it. I couldn't understand why I had been sent on such a wild goose chase. Early next morning we left without eating any breakfast, and hurried back home to see what was happening there.

"Meanwhile, Phulmaya had gathered together twelve other ladies, and they went to the church building to pray for us during the evening. While they were there, a crowd of about 200 students from nearby schools and colleges surrounded them, armed with axes, knives and sticks. They were looking for me. They were led by a student leader, a *magar*, but I don't think he was the mastermind. He was more of a stooge for the *panchayat* bigwigs. There had just been a referendum about whether to bring in multi-party democracy, and the voting was 54% to 46% to keep the appointed *panchayats*. Now, secret orders were going out to destroy the Christians.

"Anyway, the student leader bragged they would carve me up with their knives, press salt into the wounds, and parade me round the district as a dreadful warning to the others and a humiliation to the church. They thought I was inside the church but I was off on my wild goose chase. So they set fire to the church and beat up the women as they came out. Both Phulmaya and our daughter Rumar were quite seriously beaten. But the fire went out and the church was still usable!

"When I got back the following day, my next door neighbour, who was not a Christian, warned me what was happening and gave me some money to enable me to run away immediately. Over the next few hours, seven other people came to me and warned me that the crowd was going to return and destroy the houses of the Christians. I had to flee for my life. The last man came at three in the morning. 'Either run away or go to the police station for sanctuary. You'll be safe there. Otherwise, you'll be killed.'

"One of the informants seemed to know more than the others. 'They've planned a secret date with the Chief District Officer to destroy all the Christians in Nawalparaisi. They'll burn all the churches and the houses of Christians, and kill as many as possible. The date is 20th January.' This was the following Sunday, when we would all be in church. We always met on Sundays, even though in Nepal Saturday is the day off and the town churches meet on Saturdays. Our people were all farmers, so it didn't matter. We only changed to Saturdays a year or two ago.

"So I'd been given inside information about how they planned to get rid of the Christians. It was like Mordecai finding out what Haman and the others were up to in the book of Esther. When the Jews found out there was a day planned to slaughter them, they fasted and prayed. So I thought we ought to be doing the same. But, apart from that, I really wasn't sure what to do. I asked Phulmaya, 'Do I stay, flee or try the police post?' We prayed about it for a couple of hours, and then, at 5am, I heard what seemed like a voice inside my head. It said, 'Go to the police station and learn a lesson from there.' It seemed right to take a friend with me again, so I knocked up Lal Bahadur. He was a retired Gurkha captain from the Indian army, and I thought he might be useful. We cycled together down to the main road, then caught an early bus to the police station.

"As we got off the bus, we bumped straight into the police chief, who was walking down the road to work. I felt he wanted to arrest me straightaway, but I was saved because he was a good friend of Captain Lal. 'A mob have beaten up his wife and daughter and set his church on fire. They are looking for him to kill him. The Christians don't do any harm. They pray for the nation, they're not traitors. You must protect him,' implored Lal. But the police chief shook his head. 'We can't help the Christians even if we want to because we've had orders to destroy them. It's not just local this time. It's everywhere! We've got authority to eliminate them ourselves if the mobs don't get them first. If this man were alone, I'd have arrested him by now, but the written orders haven't arrived yet, so I'll let you take your friend away for the moment.'

"Lal said, 'It's much too dangerous to stay around here. We thought it would be safe with the police but it seems there's nowhere safe in this world. Let's get the bus straight back.' At that moment, a bus arrived going in the right direction and we got on. Lal sat down but I was too upset and agitated even to sit. There was nowhere left to go, they were after us over the whole country. I kept praying as the bus trundled back but in my heart I felt defeated. 'Lord, is this the end of your kingdom here and the end of my ministry? Surely there is nothing left for me to do than go back home and be killed! Lord, what do I do? I can wait for you to act, save myself somehow, or just give up.' I felt like giving up.

"The bus had gone 4 kilometres and it was rumbling over one of the metal bridges that make such a noise. Suddenly, I saw a Bible verse, all brightly lit up and written out straight in front of my eyes. It wasn't just something in my mind—it was as big and bright and real as a bonfire. If God was wanting to say something to me, he couldn't have done it more obviously. The verse was Esther 4:14. The words were Mordecai's when he persuaded Queen Esther to speak up and save the Jews before they were all done to death on the appointed day by Haman:

> If you remain silent at this time, relief and deliverance for the Jews will arise from another place, but you and your father's family will perish. And who knows but that you have come to royal position for such a time as this?

"The verse calmed my nerves. Perhaps God was going to deliver us in one way or another. And perhaps I was in the position I was in for such a time as this. I was the one who knew what was planned, both from my informant last night and from the police chief, and I was the leader the other Christians would listen to. Today was Wednesday and the student leader was getting his troops ready to burn us out and kill the church leaders on Sunday. Esther, Mordecai and the Jews fasted and prayed for three days before Esther went to the king to beg for their lives. There were still three days for us to fast and pray before the planned action.

"We got off the bus and cycled back to Lal's house. I was beginning to see what to do, but I was still shocked and depressed. The others couldn't cheer me up even though they tried.

"That night I had a vision. You can tell the difference between an ordinary dream and a vision, and this was a vision. There was a very deep and darkly threatening river in a gorge, and against the bank was a huge rock, steep and craggy, reaching from the river up to the very top of the gorge. I saw myself at the bottom, then slowly climbing step by perilous step up the rock, away from the river, and towards safety. And a verse came to me in the vision:

The Lord is my rock, my fortress and my deliverer; my God is my rock, in whom I take refuge.

Psalm 18:2

"Next morning, I went home and gathered together as many Church leaders as I could. Some of the men had already fled into the jungle, but I gathered eighteen leaders and we went into the jungle together. We took no food, just black tea. As we fasted, we studied the book of Esther. The next day, Friday, we walked together up the biggest hill in the area. It's about 10 kilometres away and about 2000 metres high. We carried on studying Esther, fasting and praying that God would save the lives of the Christians in the area and protect our homes and churches. Now we had a wonderful vantage point from which to see what the student leader's mobs would do on Sunday. You can see the whole of the area from the top of this hill, all our churches and houses were spread out on the plain below us. Beyond our area we could see the huge river Narayani and the Chitwan National Park where the tourists go to see the rhinos, elephants and tigers.

"Sunday morning came and we kept an anxious lookout. Where would the first flames come from? All morning we watched. The sun climbed higher, peaked and started to go down again. There was still nothing to be seen. We couldn't understand it. Finally, at 3pm we could take no more. We decided we would have to go to Barataidi and find out what was going on.

"It took a few hours to get there, but, as we approached we heard the sound of singing coming from the church. As we got nearer we could hardly believe that the church was still standing. What's more, it was packed with people and they were all singing. We ran up to them. 'Has nothing happened here yet?' we asked, full of anxiety. 'No, nothing,' they replied. 'The student leader was down by the main road last night, gathering a huge crowd together ready to attack us today. He was working them up into a mob. He can't have been paying attention to the road, because he was knocked down and killed by a truck. The mob panicked, ran away and dispersed.'"

In the way he was talking, Lok was conveying the excitement and elation of the moment, but also the awe and gravity in the way they were rescued. When Esther and her people had fasted for three days, she went to the king and changed his mind. Haman plotted to kill Mordecai on the appointed day by hanging him on a great public gallows he had erected for the purpose. But in the end it was Haman who was executed on his own gallows, and his body was left there hanging on display, a terrible warning of the consequences of opposing the Living God.

"I never understood why," added Lok, "but the student leader's body was just left there by the roadside for three days for everyone to see before, finally, the police removed it. Everyone in the area must have seen it. God had told me to go to the police station to learn a lesson. I'd learnt it from Esther. In time of peril, we must fast and pray, do the things He's given us to do, and leave God to do the rest. And I'd learnt afresh the awesome truth of Hebrews 10:31

> It is a dreadful thing to fall into the hands
> of the living God.

CHAPTER 10

BATTLE HONOURS

Lok was surviving every threat against him. God seemed determined to build His church, and sweep opposition away. But was there something special about Nepal that, despite terrible threats, the persecutors never in the end quite killed the Christians? After all, there are many martyrs elsewhere.

"We've survived because God has looked after us. But also there is something inside many Nepalis, especially the Mongolian and Tibetan tribes like the Tamangs. It's called '*daya*'. It doesn't have a direct translation into English, but 'mercy' is about the nearest. So, sometimes they pull back from the brink, and sometimes non-Christians have helped us because they have *daya* inside them. But Christians have been murdered by caste Hindus, and there was a young teacher in Dhading near where I was born who was beaten to death by Tamangs. So it does happen here."

But how was it that the God of love that the Nepali Christians embraced so enthusiastically was also a God of such terrible judgement on their opponents?

By the 1980s, the people in Nawalparaisi were becoming Christians by the hundreds, often because they discovered that God loved them. He wasn't like the old gods, always ready to judge and punish. Through Jesus, He was always ready to forgive. This God of love was being discovered both through answered prayers for healing, and through the superhuman love shown by Christians. But at the same time, this God of love seemed to be sending the church's enemies to early graves. Where was the love in that? Isn't God supposed to love everybody?

This was not a problem to the Nepali Christians, because they experienced the same God of both love and judgement that they found in the Bible. Haman was hanged, and many other opponents of God's people were killed with him. Judas committed suicide. Ananias and Sapphira died at a word from Peter. Herod died a nasty death in Caesarea. Bar Jesus was blinded by Paul. The Gospel of Love that Jesus preached was the love of forgiveness offered to all. But those who rejected or opposed the Gospel remained unforgiven and under judgement:

The God for whom sin didn't matter, who wouldn't hurt a fly and who would let his human opponents trample all over him may figure in the Western liberal imagination, but he didn't figure in the experience of Nepali Christians. He is not to be found in the Bible and so had not been thought of in Nepal."

For God so loved the world that he gave his one and only Son, that whoever believes in him shall not perish but have eternal life Whoever believes in him is not condemned, but whoever does not believe stands condemned already because he has not believed in the name of God's one and only Son. Whoever believes in the Son has eternal life, but

whoever rejects the Son will not see life, for God's wrath
remains on him.

John 3:16,18,36

Although Lok's list of battle honours was growing, there
always seemed a new battle to follow the one just won.
Even after the death of the student leader, Lok could still
not get the feeling of dread out of his system. They had been
saved from the mob, but the police chief had said they
would have to destroy them if the mob didn't get them first.

"I decided to spend the whole night praying about the
situation. Towards the end of the night, I saw a vision of
more persecution. People surrounded our house with burning logs and I was upstairs looking for water to put the fire
out. But there was far too little, and all I could do was
sprinkle a little on the flames, quite ineffectually. Then I
took a friend up the nearby mountain to pray. There my
friend had a vision of a great wheat farm, well irrigated,
producing a massive harvest. I had a vision of eight people
being arrested, and one escaping while seven were jailed.
So perhaps the future held both persecution and growth for
the church.

"A few days later, I had to go to Kathmandu for a
meeting of NCF. I caught the bus in the late morning. At
1pm, six policemen arrived in the village with orders to
arrest the Christian men. I was top of the list. As usual, they
left the women alone. Eight other men on the list were
arrested, and the police stripped everything out of the
church. They left it an empty shell. One of the eight got out
quickly with a bribe, but the other seven were all sent to jail
for six years.

"But I was the main target and they had missed me. They couldn't understand how I had slipped through their fingers again. They only decided to go to Barataidi at the last minute. There was no way I could have known they were coming. I think I was beginning to be something of a legend. I got the news in Kathmandu. Three of the main church leaders in Kathmandu came back with me to support me, but the police had all gone and things had quietened down. Perhaps the police had got busy with other things and didn't have the time to chase me. So I was able to stay at home.

"A month later, my father died. He had lived quietly with us for years, keeping his faith. He worked the land with us and occasionally he went back to Pokhara to work as a porter and get cash in hand. But now I had a real practical problem. I had to give him a proper Christian burial, but most of the village would expect his body to be burned by the *lama*. People called on me to threaten me and make me conform to the tribal traditions. So one night, I got my friend, Dhan Lal, to help me and we took my father's body out into the jungle secretly, and there we buried him.

"A week went by and I was beginning to think it was the end of the matter. But then, very early one morning, the police called. They were backed up by a crowd of about a hundred people. There had been a complaint. The *lama* had not been brought in and given the body in the proper way. At that moment, a visitor arrived at the house. She was a Japanese doctor I had met at a hospital in Tansen. She slipped in and hid upstairs, but the crowd had spotted her. They turned their attention to her and started screaming, 'She must be the foreigner who brought this alien religion to us. Bring her out and we'll kill her. Then you'll have to keep to the customs!'

"The shouting went on altogether for four and a half hours. The crowd bellowed at me to exhume my father and arrange the customary cremation with a rice and buffalo sacrifice. I refused, so they said, 'Give us the rice and buffalo and we'll do it ourselves'.

"'I'm a Christian', I replied, 'So I did for my father what was right according to the Bible. I'll not give you any rice or buffalo. Just leave our visitor alone, and do whatever you want to me!' The crowd began to argue among themselves. 'We sent those seven to gaol, but this man is even ready to die. What advantage would there be in killing him? He still wouldn't have conformed. We'll just have to leave him, we can't do a thing with him!' So, one by one, rather like the crowd wanting to stone the woman caught in adultery, they went away, and the doctor and I were saved.

"That evening I went down to the main road and bumped into one of the men from the crowd. He was calm and alone by now. I took him to a tea shop and bought him a drink. Then he told me the plan they had hatched after they left us. The ringleader was the village priest and biggest land-owner. They were going to capture me, strip me, put a *tika* mark on my forehead, and march me round the village to humiliate me. Then they were going to make me drink the blood of a goat offered to an idol and then worship the idol itself. If I resisted they would beat me up and kill me.

"I returned up the hill to Phulmaya, despondent. There seemed no end to the threats and the crises. All the other Christian men in the area were now in prison or had fled. Only the women were left for me to talk things over with. I felt I couldn't go on like this and might as well accept that I was going to die soon. 'But even if I am going to die, I should still carry on sharing the Gospel,' I decided, grimly.

"That night, I read a book called, 'Christian Martyrs'. In it was the story of an early Christian who was ordered to worship an idol. Instead, he went straight round to the idol and smashed it up. 'That's it,' I said to myself, 'if they want a fight, I'll give them one, I'll collect the village idols the priest operates and break them up. I'm ready to die anyway, so I've nothing to lose.'

"The idols were in a grove of trees. Next morning, I went round the village, shouting at the top of my voice, 'I'm off to destroy the idols that scandalous priest operates to make money out of you.' The priest had a weak point, and I had found it. 'The man's a scandal, living with his uncle's wife, no one should be following him!' I got round all the people who might be part of his lynch mob. By the time I'd finished, I'd turned them all against him. I didn't even need to go and destroy the idols themselves, I had destroyed their power.

"But things were still serious. The families of the men in gaol were penniless and near to starving. I visited one family, who were all at home, crying, and I felt responsible. After all, I was the one who had persuaded them to become Christians in the first place. So, I collected a lawyer and wrote out two applications to pay the very large fines that would get the men out of gaol. I would need to sell all my land, but I could just do it. Then I went down to the law courts with my land deeds.

"It was a very big mistake."

CHAPTER 11

ENOUGH EVIDENCE TO CONVICT YOU ?

"The courtroom was at the District HQ in Paraisi. I got there on 7th May 1981, a month before the monsoon, so it was very hot. It was a surprisingly small room, brick-built but plastered, on an upper floor of the building. The judge sat really high up on a podium at the front. Three court officers and my solicitor sat underneath the judge, looking at the rest of us. I stood looking back at them, flanked on either side by police officers. There was drinking water available, but I was not allowed to use it. I had to stand to attention like that for an hour and a half. The judge was a Newar, all dressed up in his *Dhaka Topee* hat worn point upwards, and his official Nepali suit like they wear in parliament, all made out of the most expensive material. The suit had long brown pants, baggy at the top and skin-tight below the knee, and a brown shirt, tied at the front. And, let us say he was amply proportioned.

"He read through the land deed application my solicitor had handed to him. The other copy had gone to the gaoler. If they both signed it, then I lost my land but the seven Christians would be released from prison. He read through the land deed. Then he looked down at me, and I looked up at him. Our eyes met. He was so high up I was getting a crick in my neck. He put his head in the land deed again. Then he looked at me again. And I looked at him. Then he looked at the land deed. Then at me. He was getting puzzled and agitated. At long last, he spoke. 'How many Lok Bahadur Tamangs in Barataidi?' 'Just one, me,' I replied. He peered over the podium and looked me up and down yet again. I suppose I was a pitiful sight. I was desperately thin at the time. We'd had so much trouble that we weren't spending enough time cultivating our land, so we were going hungry. I also had the worry of the persecution and the grief at my father's death. The vest I was wearing was full of holes. I couldn't afford a proper shirt, and I was wearing pretty small shorts.

"'You?!' he blurted out. 'You—the notorious Christian leader?!' he shouted, incredulously. He'd obviously believed the propaganda that Christian leaders were all financed from the West and were extremely wealthy. 'Are you sure you're Lok Bahadur Tamang the Christian?' 'Yes, that's me.' He leaned over to the clerk of the court, sitting below him. 'Go and fetch me the police file on Lok Bahadur Tamang the Christian.'

"The clerk was away quite a while, but eventually he struggled in, someone else helping him, with a very heavy file. The podium groaned under its weight. Later, my solicitor told me there were 111 different reports in it, each one a different complaint about my illegal Christian activities."

Lok was really enjoying remembering the story. "There's a question we ask Christians in England," I said, laughing. "'If you were on trial for being a Christian, would there be enough evidence to convict you?' I'm afraid some of us might be found not guilty, but you sound like an open and shut case!"

"Yes, I'm afraid the evidence for me being a Christian was pretty overwhelming. Part of it was that when all the other Christians had been in court for their trials, their defence was to blame me. I was the one who persuaded them to become Christians, and they were just the small fry. They were saying that they became Christians when I healed the sick, but they didn't know a lot about the details of the faith themselves. It was the best defence they had, and every time it got added to my file.

"By now, my application to use my land to pay the fines to get the others out of gaol, had been forgotten. It was as though I was on trial, and I was obviously expected to explain myself. Fortunately, I had a promise from Jesus:

> They will lay hands on you and persecute you. They will deliver you to synagogues and prisons, and you will be brought before kings and governors, and all on account of my name. This will result in your being witnesses to them. But make up your mind not to worry beforehand how you will defend yourselves. For I will give you words and wisdom that none of your adversaries will be able to resist or contradict.
>
> *Luke 21:12-15*

"So I told the judge my life story, explaining why I was a Christian, the things God did, and what had happened to me recently. The judge listened in fascinated silence. By the end, he finally had to believe I really was the great Lok Bahadur Tamang, the most wanted Christian in the District, the legend who always escaped the clutches of the mob and the police.

"'Lok Bahadur Tamang', he said eventually, 'if either I or the gaoler signs this paper then we'll have to put you in gaol. We'd have no option. You're the most wanted Christian in the District, and we couldn't explain that we just let you go when the paperwork showed we had you in our hands. I won't sign it for the moment, but if the gaoler has signed it, you've had it! But we've never met a man like you before. You're obviously honest and sincere, and if your God is real and your Jesus is your saviour, he won't have let the gaoler sign the paper. We've been here for an hour and a half already, so he ought to have signed it ages ago. Let's find out. Clerk! Go and fetch the documents from the gaoler!'

"The clerk went off again, and my fate hung in the balance. A few minutes later, he returned with the documents. 'Here they are—he never signed them,' he said, handing them up to the judge. The judge broke into smiles and clapped out loud. 'The ones in prison all blamed you, but you're an honest man. They'll get out in due course, but you had better go home now!' The judge got down off his podium, gave me back my land documents, hurried me outside and personally put me into an auto-rickshaw.

"Two months later, I was able to take someone else's land deeds to buy the prisoners out. One or two had turned from the faith, but the others had held firm and returned to the church."

CHAPTER 12

SCATTER THE SLUMS

The persecution in 1980 was much more widespread than before. While it was happening, many people became Christians, and lots of churches were born. The persecution seemed to have the opposite result of that intended.

"There were three main reasons why persecuting us was counter productive. Firstly, persecution forces the real Christians to pray, often fervently and sometimes desperately. We would get together and pray all night. Prayer is an important weapon in spiritual warfare. God answered our prayers. Sometimes we prayed for power to witness to our faith through our persecution, sometimes we simply prayed for people to become Christians. So prayer became the powerhouse of the church and its growth.

"Secondly, it wasn't only the judge who was impressed by our sincerity and courage. The other Christians were following my example—courage is infectious. They were going to maintain their witness whatever happened. Philippians 2:14-16 is very important to me when there is persecution:

> Do everything without complaining or arguing, so that you may become blameless and pure, children of God without fault in a crooked and depraved generation, in which you shine like stars in the universe as you hold out the word of life—in order that I may boast on the day of Christ that I did not run or labour for nothing.

"So the Christians did their best not to grumble or question when the world seemed evil, but tried hard to live blameless lives, helping and loving their neighbours, not quarrelling and getting drunk, but shining like stars in front of them. When Christians behave well under persecution they make Christianity very attractive.

"But they also make people wild with curiosity. This is the third thing. 'What's it all about? They don't drink but they seem very happy. It must be important to them because they'll go to gaol rather than give it up. When they pray for the sick they get better. They say they've got good news to share.' So, as well as being impressed, people become curious to learn about Jesus. They wanted for themselves this joyful, powerful faith that's worth suffering for.

"Also in 1980, the Nepal Church Fellowship began to get more organised. We had to if we were to cope with the national problem of persecution and the rapid growth. Fifty church leaders had a conference in Pokhara where we devised a national strategy for evangelism. We prayed together non-stop for 178 hours, sleeping in relays. At the end of that time, the Holy Spirit spoke through one of the women delegates—'Now is the time to preach the Gospel through the whole of Nepal from east to west, from north to south.' So we divided the country up between us.

"I was given Manang, up in the Himalayas, to evangelise. I took a small team with me, but it was already November when we got there, and beginning to get cold. We all
lived on the Terai where it's never really cold and we didn't
have adequate clothing. We had to leave, beaten by the
weather! So we went instead to the middle hills among the
Tamangs in Dhading, Gorkha and Lamjung. It was a much
more natural place for us to go and it was very fruitful."
Lok shivered and held himself tight as he remembered
being seriously cold in Manang.

"I've noticed that before," I remarked to Lok, smiling at
human frailties. "No matter how hard church leaders try to
follow the Holy Spirit we still get the details wrong and
leave ourselves out in the cold! What a good job He always
gives us another chance."

"After all that," Lok continued, "large numbers of people started seeking me out in Barataidi wanting to learn how
to become Christians. I became a sort of one man training
college. The only trouble was, I had no formal training
myself! But one or two individuals helped me and sent me
Bible study materials and sermon notes so I could learn
while I was teaching.

"Then in 1982, I had a vision. It was warning me about
a future problem. The vision had just six words in it—'The
Government will scatter the slums". I didn't know what it
meant, but I kept my eyes open. Then in April, I heard of a
new Government edict. Not all the people who moved
down from the hills to Nawalparaisi did it officially with
land papers, like me. Some had just arrived and squatted on
land. Many of them had been there for years. In the thirty-
seven *panchayats* on our side of the big hill, they wanted
to move 3000 people off the land they had occupied. This

included eighty-six families from Barataidi, thirty of whom were Christians. They wanted to evict most of the village, and practically the entire church!

"For eight months I kept going to Kathmandu time and time again to lobby civil servants and Government ministers and try to stop them destroying these homes and evicting the people. Suddenly, I was no longer just the church leader, I was speaking on behalf of the whole community, most of whom were still Hindus. In the end, I couldn't stop the Government evicting the people, destroying their houses, and re-allocating the land, but I did persuade them to offer the people new land somewhere else when it came up, and somewhere to stay in the meantime.

"All the Christian families accepted the Government offer I'd negotiated, but some of the Hindus didn't. They were too suspicious of me and treated me like an enemy even though I'd done all this for them. So they lost everything.

"The people were moved to three camps or townships on the sand and rocky flood plain of a big river about 80km to the west. They were called Pipalpate, Narsahi, and Rewareta. The people stayed there for two years, supported by food aid the Government had negotiated from Israel.

"Ten Christian families had gone to each of the three townships. I went to visit them and take meetings. I encouraged them to start evangelism. But back home it was terrible. The only people left in Barataidi were my family and about ten Hindu families who had all got land papers. For the first few years, I was the only Christian in the area, now my family were the only Christians left. I worried about how the Christians would get on in exile by the river bank. I felt that my life's work, my labours and persecutions, had gone up in smoke. My church had disappeared. The Hindus gossiped about me—'Lok Bahadur doesn't go to church any more—he must have given up being a Christian!' I was yearning to go to church, but there was no one left to meet with me.

"I had offers from Pokhara and Tansen and other places to pastor churches there, but I didn't feel it was right to move. We were half starving in Barataidi, though, because there was no income from the church and the local economy was in ruins because most of the people had left. I spent three months in mourning, despairing at events and thinking I would never again be a pastor.

"I was broken hearted, but God's route to new life often seems to be through crucifixion. At the end of three months, I built a room on the side of the house to use for prayer. It was small, but I saw it as a symbol of hope for the future. Then Phulmaya and I decided to start a new fellowship, using the new room. I put out twelve mats on the floor and they filled the room. So it was just big enough for twelve people to sit and pray. Then we waited for Sunday morning. We decided to hold the service at 11am prompt even if no one came to join us. We didn't do much advertising and we didn't really expect anyone else to come. Instead, we spent the time praying, waiting for instructions from God. Early on Sunday morning, God gave us a word from Isaiah 61:1ff. It leapt out and overwhelmed us. Its amazing and far reaching promises all seemed to be for us:

> The Spirit of the Sovereign Lord is upon me, because the Lord has anointed me to preach good news to the poor. He has sent me to bind up the broken-hearted, to proclaim the year of the Lord's favour and the day of vengeance of our God, to comfort all who mourn, and provide for those who grieve in Zion—to bestow on them a crown of beauty

instead of ashes, the oil of gladness instead of mourning, and a garment of praise instead of despair. They will be called oaks of righteousness, a planting of the Lord for the display of his splendour.

"At this point, I heard the Lord say to me, 'Lok Bahadur, you are a mature tree, a strong oak with deep roots. You are not going to get blown over by a gale.' It was true I'd been shaken, but what God said to me then gave me a whole new confidence that has never left me. But there was more:

They will rebuild the ancient ruins and restore the places long devastated; they will renew the ruined cities that have been devastated for generations. Aliens will shepherd your flocks; foreigners will work your fields and vineyards. And you will be called priests of the Lord, you will be named ministers of our God. You will feed on the wealth of nations, and in their riches you will boast. Instead of their shame my people will receive a double portion, instead of disgrace they will rejoice in their inheritance; and so they will inherit a double portion in their land, and everlasting joy will be theirs. For I, the Lord, love justice; I hate robbery and iniquity. In my faithfulness I will reward them and make an everlasting covenant with them. Their descendants will be known among the nations and their offspring among the peoples. All who see them will acknowledge that they are a people the Lord has blessed. As the soil makes the young plant come up and a garden causes seed to grow, so the Sovereign Lord will make righteousness and praise spring up before all nations.

"As we sat, half starved and alone, praying amid the devastation of Barataidi, the promises were staggering. God had planted us there as oaks of righteousness and we were not to leave. We were strong and mature enough to survive. We were to have praise and gladness instead of mourning. The ruins will be rebuilt. Prosperity will come again. I will again be called a minister of the Lord. The wealth of nations will help feed us. We and our spiritual children will become well known among the nations of the world. God will use us to cause righteousness and praise to spring up all over the world.

"How all this was going to happen, we had no idea. But I knew straight away that from now on I had to be involved in development work. I had to rebuild and restore prosperity for all the people of Barataidi and the surrounding area, whether they were Christians or not. It seemed like a direct command.

"And then it was 11 o'clock."

CHAPTER 13

YOU WILL FEED ON THE WEALTH OF NATIONS

"On the dot of 11, eleven people turned up from the next door village and filled our new room. They were carrying a sick woman so there was exactly one person for each mat. I taught them for a while, and we began some worship. We prayed for the sick lady and she got better. The next week twenty people turned up with another sick lady, and she was healed as well. Soon after, some Tharus came and brought a third sick lady. The Tharus are the original tribal inhabitants of the Terai. At that time hardly any of them were Christians. Their lady was healed too. Within two months I was forced to build a much bigger building holding ninety people. A nurse from Norway who was working in Nepal gave me some money for it, so already Isaiah was coming true—the wealth of the nations was helping to rebuild Barataidi. In October 1983 we held a conference for a hundred and sixty people. The second building was already too small even though it was brand new.

"Meanwhile, wonderful things were going on among the exiles down by the banks of the river. I visited them when I could and at first I worried whether the Christians would manage to keep their faith. But there were ten Christian families in each of the three places. That was enough for them to support one another and to start a church. The old church had died when the people were moved, but it had given birth to triplets! It was like when the Christians in the first church in Jerusalem were scattered to Judea and Samaria by the persecution when Stephen was stoned. The Holy Spirit had pushed them out so that the church could grow.

"After a while, some of the new Christians from the river valley began trickling back to the thirty seven *panchayats* our side of the big hill. As soon as they arrived, they started sharing their faith. A new wave of fellowships started to spring up. Two years after the scattering many of the people were given land in the forty *panchayats* on the other side of the big hill. The same thing happened there.

"Now on our side of the hill alone there are about fifty churches and 10,000 believers who have all come from the thirty families who were sent to the squatter camps by the river.

"We'd never had any foreign money or aid from overseas in our village, though it seemed to be getting through to other places. I knew I had to see what I could do about it. One day in 1984 I was down in Rajhar, the town that was growing as a centre for the area because it was on flat land by the road. I noticed an American lady who was working with the 'Women's Development Association'. She was with a Nepali lady officer-in-charge and a chap from the bank.

"I followed them to see what they were up to and discovered they were helping Tharus who lived south of Rajhar with soft loans to purchase livestock and other development projects. They were also setting up adult literacy and tailoring classes. I followed them around for the whole day, but they ignored me. Because there were some Brahmins around, and I'm too low caste for them to associate with, the officer lady had to ignore me as well, or she would have had trouble. I think they might also have known I was a Christian. Anyway, I followed them for the whole of the next day as well. On the third day, four or five little children of daily labourers who had trickled back from Pipalpate by the river came with me. They were used to hanging around me.

"That day, the American lady, whose name I discovered was Peggy, was giving out seeds. There are four Village Development Areas (*panchayats*) in our district and during the day she gave out seeds in three of them. The children and I followed her round. Eventually, I was able to say to her, 'I'm from Barataidi ward. You're giving out seeds to the other three wards in our area but not to us. Can't you include us as well?'

"Peggy went off and talked to the others, so I listened in. They obviously weren't interested because I was a Christian. They claimed our ward was outside their development map. They showed her the map and they had drawn us outside the area on purpose. They knew there were Christians in our *panchayat*. Peggy whispered to me to come back tomorrow.

"So, on the fourth day I went back to find them, with the children in tow again. I took Peggy off for a cup of tea at a tea shop. She started chatting to the children. 'What's your name?' 'Rebecca'. 'And what's your name?' 'John'. She went all wide-eyed and said, 'Are you Christians?' The children said they were, and I explained that that was why we had been left off the map. Peggy said, 'I'm not a Christian, but I did go to Sunday School. This is not fair. I'll help you.'

"I explained to her that the help must be for all the people in Barataidi, Hindus as much as Christians. It was filling up again as new settlers arrived, and squatters began to trickle back in. Some of them were very poor and there were great needs. I wanted there to be unity in the village. Aid shouldn't be divisive. Sometimes Christians get accused of only being Christians for the money we can get from foreigners. People like that get called 'Rice Christians'. I didn't want any Rice Christians in Barataidi.

"Peggy promised we would hear from her, and, sure enough, there were all sorts of evaluations done on us in the following weeks. Then help began to arrive from various international groups.

"Over the next five years we had development help in the form of loans for rearing goats for meat, a re-afforestation scheme, vegetable seeds, fruit trees, adult literacy classes, including books and blackboards, a nursery and school, pay for teachers, fencing to keep wild animals out of the farms, sewing machines and tailoring classes. By 1988 Peggy had gone, but she linked us with Nelly from the Dutch aid group SNV (Society of Netherlands Volunteers). She found us a grant for a large pond from which we could irrigate and grow rice. The total cost over the five years was about 6 *lakhs* (£6000). I know because I was keeping the accounts.

"£6000 may not seem a lot to Westerners, but it seems a vast sum when you are poor. And money goes a lot further in Nepal than in the West. My dogged persistence over four days had paid off. The word from Isaiah had come true. We were feeding on the wealth of many nations."

CHAPTER 14

THE FOREST AND
THE FLOOR

Lok and I found a taxi in the cool of dawn. He was disgusted with the driver for asking Rs 90 for the trip. "Don't worry, they always ask me Rs 200 when I'm by myself," I laughed. And so we rattled down the hill to the long distance bus station.

Lok had business in Barataidi and I was tagging along. It was about the Community Forest. The Government had turned forest management over to the local communities. Barataidi's Community Forest provides fodder for the goats, buffalo and other animals, fuel for the kitchen fires and timber when needed. Lok has done the annual accounts and now he needs to meet the auditor and call a village meeting to have the accounts approved before lodging them at the District Office in Paraisi.

But there is another and more serious problem. Lok and about thirteen other families living at the top end of the village all have land papers. But the eighty families living at the bottom end of the village, who have come in since the clearance of 1983, do not. Legally, they are squatting. An influential group have made a legal application to evict the eighty families and gain control of the whole of Barataidi's Community Forest for themselves. Most of the eighty are Tamangs, and nearly half of them are Christians. Lok has been fighting a legal battle for months to get the land the eighty are on registered in their name and to keep the forest. If they are evicted, it will be a repeat of 1983. Lok himself will be isolated and surrounded, excluded from his own forest resources.

The man who has to make the decision is the District Forestry Officer. Lok thinks he is a fair man who is on his side. But powerful local figures have threatened the Officer with the sack if he gives the land to the Tamang Christians. They have also told Lok that, if he wins the case on behalf of his people, they will have him beaten up. The DFO should have made the decision while Lok was telling me about the last time the slums were scattered. Lok's church, apparently, were fasting and praying about it while we were talking in Pokhara.

Lok needs to know the outcome because, if he has won, he may need to avoid going home, or at least shorten his visit. People will be after him. If he has lost, he'll be safe but all the landless people of Barataidi will be removed.

Lok telephoned for news the previous day. It seemed to me that the DFO was between a rock and a hard place. He was likely to use delaying tactics. Lok had come back smiling. "He hasn't made a decision. It's safe for us to go in the morning."

The large bus station was crowded with buses preparing to leave on the Mugling road for Kathmandu or the Terai.

We soon found our bus because its number had been scribbled on the ticket. It steadily filled with passengers. A taxi arrived with a seriously ill patient laid out on the back seat. She was connected to drips and looked in a bad way. Why she was leaving hospital in Pokhara in this state I couldn't work out. Tenderly her helpers carried her out of the taxi on to the front seat of the bus where another lady was to travel with her, squatting down in the aisle next to her. Now the bus was an ambulance as well.

When we were full, the engine was revved, the horn was blown and about twenty more people appeared from no-where, clambering aboard as we began to move. As we drove through the suburbs we stopped a few more times to pick up passengers until there was no more standing room. If you do not like your personal space invaded, do not travel on a Nepali bus. The man behind me was leaning forward on my seat back so that I hit my head on his hands if I jerked back half an inch. The people standing in the aisle leaned over on top of me and stood on my foot which was pushed out into the aisle by my rucksack on the floor between my legs. The people crushed into the space in front of me by the front entrance threatened to fall over on to me. At the slightest stop, street hawkers stuck their heads in the win-dow or pushed their way through the crowd, all wanting to sell to the white man. The air was full of vigorous debate about I knew not what, but the man who had brought his goat with him did not seem popular. In this lively state, we bounced and shook our way across Nepal's stunning scen-ery for hour after endless hour. A Nepali bus ride is an experience in life you will never forget. I loved it.

In one town, a sorry looking barefoot boy hopped on with his mother, and squashed in among the standing passengers just next to me. He was on one leg because the other had large sores and it looked like a growth of some sort had just been removed at an outpatients' clinic. He was obviously in a lot of pain, and grimaced horribly when people brushed past his leg. I invited him to sit on my knee and he grinned at me. I held him round the middle with my hands, but not too tight because I could feel every rib under his shirt. He was so flimsy I felt as though I could crush his rib cage. I fed him biscuits from my rucksack and he ate them as though they were caviar.

At the town of Narayanghat, our bus finally left the hill country and turned south west for the Indian border through the Terai. Not long now to Rajhar. Soon we slowed down because all manner of stopped vehicles were littering the road. We picked our way around them and kept on going. Then I saw the ford. It was across a hundred yards of river bed which an hour ago had been bone dry and would soon be so again. But there had just been a downpour and the river was suddenly a raging torrent. A car was stuck in it and looked as though it was going to be swept away. People were desperately trying to save it. As we drove through I could feel the sideways pressure of the water pushing at the side of the bus and making it shudder. But we made it, and the sun was shining when we alighted at Rajhar.

We had been on the bus for seven hours and never spoken a word. No interpreter! We had, however, greatly added to our expertise in 'sign and grunt' language.

We walked the short distance to a large new church, on a track parallel to the main road about two hundred yards south of it. Friends greeted Lok and we sat down in the church building, putting on the fans for air. It was much hotter on the Terai than in Pokhara in the shadow of Machhapuchhare. There was no sign of my new interpreter, so I was still deaf and dumb. He had an even longer journey to make than me, and his bus hadn't arrived yet. I strolled around under the hot sun as it started to slide down the western sky. I bought a Coke in the bazaar. Children who were learning English at school kept trying it out on me. Just as I decided the interpreter had got lost, he turned up, coughing and tired after the trip but ready to be my ears and voice.

Meanwhile, Lok had wandered off to see a few people, but when he returned, the three of us sat down on the floor of the church together. I had an important question to ask him.

I had wanted to write about the church in Nepal ever since my first visit in 1987. Finally, in 1996 it seemed I might have an opportunity. People suggested I write about Lok Bahadur Tamang. Word came back that he would be alerted to meet me, and I flew out to Kathmandu in November. But communication in Nepal isn't always perfect, and, when I got there, the churches in Kathmandu didn't even know where he was. After a few days, a man came in from Rajhar and said he was there. So I was bundled on to a bus to meet him. I had arrived at this very church in the middle of a training week for local pastors, unannounced. Lok was nowhere to be seen. He was up in the hill villages, baptising.

However, late the next day he finally turned up, still knowing nothing about this man who had come half way round the world to ask permission to write his biography. I felt like Stanley finding Livingstone. Nervously, I put to him what I wanted to do. "Oh good," replied Lok, "We need this. Let's sit down and start". And so for a few days in Rajhar in 1996 we talked and got to know each other and arranged for me to return later to finish the job. I had slept on the floor of the church with only a wafer thin mat between my sheet sleeping bag and the solid concrete. After a few nights of this I had seriously bruised ribs and ached all over.

So, this was my important question to Lok as I crossed my legs and sat down on my old enemy the concrete floor. "Where will I be sleeping tonight?"

"Here on the church floor", replied Lok.

"Fine", I responded, brightly.

CHAPTER 15

PEACE PERFECT PEACE?

The church caretaker, Dil Bahadur, lived on site with his wife and three small children. He walked with a serious limp and the help of a stick. His hip was permanently dislocated when he was dropped as a baby by his sister. Walking was a painful business. After Lok had gone home, we ate our *dhal bhat*, and Dil finished his chores getting the church ready for the service next morning. Then we sat on the floor together to hear his story.

"I was twenty-two and I was visiting a friend's house in Barataidi. I sat on his bed as we talked and on his pillow was a book. I picked it up to look at it and saw it was a New Testament. I started reading it and I liked what I saw. I had never heard of a good God before. There are lots of Hindu names for God, lots of idols and gods, but none of them are truly good. Then I was given some Christian tracts and liked them, but I really needed someone to teach me what it all meant. I'd heard of Lok Bahadur because he comes from the same part of the Dhading hills as I do and he was the most famous Christian in the area. So I called on him. Lok explained a lot to me, he even taught me a song—'I'm looking to King Jesus'. It was the first time I had ever sung anything in my life. So I gave my life to the Lord. It was 22nd June 1977.

"I'd had an unhappy life until then. My mother died when I was two and my father when I was seventeen, and I had this hip which marked me out. My friends had someone to call 'Mum', but I didn't, and it choked me up. Also, as I grew bigger my leg got weaker and my disability more serious. So I was quite a disturbed child. I had a lot of what we call '*ashante*' but I don't think there is an English equivalent—perhaps 'unpeace' is the best. I was empty and twisted up inside mainly because I was unloved. I had never really had anyone to love me. When my father died in 1972 I moved to the Terai with my big sister. We got some *sukum basi* land. It was only then that I learnt to read and write—I'd never been to school.

"When I realised God loved me and I received the Lord into my life everything changed. Suddenly I had a great peace inside me. I was loved. That day all my anxieties and bitterness about my parents and my leg just went away and never came back. Straight away I went round and told my uncle about it and he received the Lord as well. Then I told my big sister, but it took her a few years before she believed.

"When I became a Christian, my old troubles and difficulties went for ever, and new ones came to replace them. But these new ones were from the outside and they were the kind I was happy to accept for the sake of my inner peace.

"I was baptised along with some others, but two men must have been spying on us because they reported all our names to the District HQ. Nine of us went up the big hill with Lok Bahadur for three days to pray about it, and Lok had a dream. Three bunches of thatching grass were tied together and set alight. Then they were thrown away and landed on a road where they went out. When our case came up before the Chief District Officer, he dismissed it and told the village *panchayat* to sort it out. The village head took no action and so the fire of that persecution went out as it was tossed elsewhere just like in Lok's dream.

"The second time I was arrested was on August 12th 1979. These things usually happen in the hot season when tempers are short. Six of us went to an open air market just off the east-west highway with books and tracts. We started giving out the tracts, selling the books very cheaply, and chatting to the people. But there were some police in the crowd in plain clothes. It started raining hard so I stopped selling the books. That meant I had a lot in my hands when the police came to me. 'Are you the person selling these books?' 'Yes, I am', I admitted. They took me off to talk to me so I ignored my friends and managed to walk away from them. They escaped. The police interrogated me for half-an-hour but I just said, 'I've got peace by believing in God and I want other people to know that peace as well.'

"Eventually, they took me down to the police station. I was extremely nervous and very worried, but God gave me a vision and a verse. The vision was of a mother saving her baby from falling down a well. I was the baby. God was the mother I had never had. The verse was John 14:18:

I will not leave you as orphans, I will come to you.

"I was in the police cell on remand for fifteen days. It was dirty, dark and full of mosquitos. I had no visitors, because they might have been arrested as well, and I had to feed myself using the 100 rupee note I had on me when arrested. Then I came before the magistrate and I told him about my Christian faith. He told me that if I promised to give it up and be a Hindu again he would release me immediately. I was tempted, but I remembered what Jesus had said:

Whoever acknowledges me before men, I will also acknowledge him before my Father in heaven. But whoever disowns me before men, I will disown him before my Father in heaven.

Matthew 10:32,33

"Eventually, the magistrate despaired of me, threw up his hands and said, 'What am I to do with this man?' The police took me outside for five minutes while he thought, and then I was brought back. The magistrate said, 'Dil Bahadur Tamang, because it is proved that you have been preaching the Christian faith I sentence you to six years imprisonment with only second grade rice to eat.'"

The way Dil Bahadur said those well-remembered words it was clear they were imprinted on his mind for ever. And the second grade rice seemed as heavy a blow as the six years.

"I had to put my thumb print on the sentence sheet and I was taken away to prison by a policeman. As we walked, he said to me, 'You stay in prison for six years and you'll be an old man when you come out.' That really dismayed me. But at the same time I felt I heard the Lord saying to me, 'I won't allow you to suffer any more than this, I am going through it with you.'

"Prison felt like I was in a cage—a caged animal. I wasn't even allowed out of the cell for exercise. I was completely alone, only the Lord was with me. For some reason I didn't think I would serve the whole of the six years, but I didn't know why. Eventually, after two or three weeks, Lok Bahadur came to see me, and then a few others had the courage to visit me as well. Lok said to me, 'We're going to appeal against your sentence!' The appeal took a while and went right the way up to the court in Pokhara. The church paid the costs and they got my sentence reduced to three years. After seven months in Paraisi, I was sent to Tansen prison to finish my sentence.

"The Christians in Tansen kept coming to see me and they were a wonderful encouragement to me. I left prison in 1982 with a great desire to study and evangelise. I was able to go to Nepal Bible Ashram in Kathmandu for two years and, when that finished in 1985, I joined a national evangelism campaign, going back to preach in my old village in Dhading. It's called Neber and it's 15 kilometres from the Tibetan border. I'd been back years earlier, but then they didn't understand me and thought I'd become a Muslim!

"This time, I thought I might be arrested again but God showed me some verses from 1 Peter that gave me the courage to preach:

Dear friends, do not be surprised at the painful trial you are suffering, as though something strange were happening to you. But rejoice that you participate in the sufferings of Christ, so that you may be overjoyed when his glory is revealed. If you are insulted because of the name of Christ, you are blessed, for the Spirit of glory and of God rests on you. If you suffer, it should not be as a murderer or thief or any other kind of criminal, or even as a meddler. However, if you suffer as a Christian, do not be ashamed, but praise God that you bear that name.

1 Peter 4:12-16

"On the afternoon of 3rd May, I was arrested with my brother. This time, Christians were ending up in police stations all over the country as the persecution was general. We were handcuffed and taken to the District Office. The civil servants there were fascinated by me. 'Look at this lame man. How can he do this sort of thing? He's not a thief or any other kind of criminal, he's just come here to preach his religion.' They all got together and listened to me while I explained to them what my faith meant to me. I was so happy and gave thanks to the Lord that I had the chance to tell them all about Him like that.

"They kept me for five days before I came up in court. The other prisoners were fascinated as well. 'We're here for good reasons, we deserve to be here. But you don't, you're here for no good reason at all. Yet you don't seem anxious or resentful even though you're put here unjustly. We can't weigh you up!' 'You're quite right,' I replied. 'The Lord is with me so I'm not anxious or worried at all.'"

One of the criminals being crucified with Jesus mocked him and the other one rebuked him saying:

Don't you fear God since you are under the same sentence? We are punished justly, for we are getting what our deeds deserve. But this man has done nothing wrong.

Luke 23:41

"The magistrate listened to me and had the same reaction as the one five years before, 'What am I going to do with you, Dil Bahadur?!' I replied, 'If you want to put me in prison, do so, that's fine.' He sentenced me to three years, but there was no mention of second class rice.

"After this I was only in prison for six days before Lok Bahadur arrived with some others from Pokhara. They came with bail money and they got me out. Later on, we all had to appeal in a higher court against the sentence. We lost the case again and it seemed I really was going back to prison now. But on the way to Dhading a landslide blocked the road so I gave up and went back to Barataidi. They never came looking for me and seemed to have given up the case for lack of interest! I just had to stay out of Dhading.

"When freedom came in 1990, they couldn't do anything to me any more so I was able to go back to Dhading and carry on the work. I stayed for two years and helped to establish quite a lot of new church fellowships.

"I had missed out on so many things in life—marriage, a family, a loving home life, but through all this time my verse had been Matthew 6:33:

Seek first his kingdom and his righteousness, and all these things will be given to you as well.

"Now I am married and we have three wonderful young children. I have a job as church caretaker and I lead the worship on Saturdays. My cup is full and running over. I've had all these troubles in my life, but they are to show other people that they, too, can have inner peace like mine through their own troubles."

Peace, perfect peace in this dark world of sin?
The blood of Jesus whispers 'Peace within.'

CHAPTER 16

DOES HE KNOW HE'S THE PREACHER ?

At bedtime, Dil Bahadur and his family curled up, just as they were, fully clothed, direct on the concrete floor, with no fuss, and started drifting off to sleep in blissful comfort. I gathered as many rush mats as possible, put my roll mat from England on top of the pile, and my sleeping bag on top of that. I stuffed all my clothes in my pillowcase to make a pillow. Having tried the pillow out and located a large lump, I then emptied the pillow case to remove the alarm clock from my trouser pocket.

The Dil Bahadurs seemed to perk up at this, staring wonderingly at me, but I didn't care. I remembered my ribs. It was hot, humid and therefore sweaty, so I arranged my 'mango fruity' cartons in easy reach for night time liquid and sat down on my precarious pile as far above the concrete as I could manage. They looked, wide eyed, as I slapped on the mosquito repellent, took my malaria pills, ate my multivitamin pills and swallowed my antihistamine pills for the bites. Then I had a fight with an army of ants who wished to investigate the contents of my rucksack. I won.

The children kept looking at me, mesmerised by the show. Never wishing to lower my night time standards I then changed into my Marks and Spencers pyjamas as discreetly as possible while numerous pairs of eyes looked on. I felt, in the circumstances, it was better to remove my denture after lights out. Just as I was settling, the interpreter said that I was much better placed to catch the draft from the fan than he was, so could we both move to the left three feet? I got up and started pulling my pile to the left, but it seemed to disintegrate and I had to rebuild it. I pulled the rucksack over to join me and it fell over, knocking a mango fruity carton on its side and spilling some of the precious nectar. I frantically searched for my toilet roll at the bottom of the rucksack and desperately wiped away the sweet spilt liquid before it attracted a new army of ants.

Finally, I slept and woke up without cracked ribs. I had beaten the floor!

Saturday morning! The town churches in Nepal had always met on Saturdays, the national day of rest. Lok's home church used to meet in Barataidi on a Sunday because everyone worked on the land. But, as Rajhar expanded along the main road, most of the congregation were walking for an hour to Barataidi for church. So, eighteen months ago, they had built the new one in Rajhar and closed down in Barataidi. At the same time, they moved to Saturday to accommodate the people with jobs in the town.

The congregation drifted in, trying to dodge the ferocious monsoon showers. The mats were arranged on the floor with a small gap down the centre. Men sat cross-legged on the left with the women and children on the right. People of all ages were there but there were more men than women, and the biggest group were young men and teenage boys. Dil Bahadur led the worship, using the NCF hymnbook. The singing and praying lasted about forty-five minutes. We sang Nepal's all time favourite—a Nepali translation of 'How Great Thou Art'. Nepali Christians realise there is no better place on earth to sing about the glories of creation. We sat to sing, and stood to pray, everyone praying out loud together at once. The hand of the Scots Presbyterians from Darjeeling who nurtured the first Nepali Christians was still evident, as was the influence of the charismatic revival of the 1970s. The praying out loud together had probably come from the South Korean Church.

All the time, people kept drifting in. We started with fifty and another hundred arrived late. Most of these sat near the back and were then attacked by the sidesman who half ordered and half pushed them forward to squeeze as close in to the front as possible. I thought, 'I could do with this man in my church'. But the interpreter, Lok and I sat it out at the back and he didn't dare move us.

As the worship time drew to a close, Lok whispered something to the sidesman sitting next to him, and the sidesman passed the message to the interpreter, and he whispered it to me. 'The message is,' said the interpreter, pausing for effect, 'Does he know he's the preacher?' I replied, vehemently, 'No, he doesn't!' The interpreter passed the reply up the line to Lok. A new message came the other way. I waited as it went along the chain. The interpreter leaned over and spoke out of the corner of his mouth, 'Well he is!'

I had the notices and the collection for a quick think and an emergency prayer before being beckoned to the front. A volunteer read Psalm 121 for me ('I lift up my eyes to the hills, where does my help come from? My help comes from the Lord, the Maker of heaven and earth.') while I took photos. The advantage of preaching with an interpreter is that there is plenty of time to think of the next sentence while he is interpreting the last one. The disadvantage is that you never know whether the congregation is hearing your sermon or the interpreter's. I got the definite impression mine was a good preacher in his own right. He was probably improving on my sermon as we went along.

At the end, everyone stayed and mingled. I met one or two old friends from the previous visit and played with some of the children, who all wanted their photographs taken. I chatted to Danda Lal, pastor of a daughter church. We sat on the concrete outside in the shade and he told me his story.

"One day, I was given a Christian tract. It was from the Nepali branch of an organisation called, 'Every home for Christ', and its title was, 'Are you happy?' I thought about that for a long time. No one had ever asked me that before. I'd never even asked myself. I soon realised the answer to the question was 'No'. I wasn't happy. So I opened the tract and read it. It talked about Jesus Christ who could transform lives like mine that felt pointless, unhappy and oppressed by fears. He could save me from the state I was in and give me purpose and love.

"I was so seriously impressed that I decided I wanted to become a Christian and take my chance of happiness. But

I didn't know any Christians at all to go and talk to. I thought about what to do. The only Christian I had ever heard of was Lok Bahadur Tamang. Everyone knew about him. He was notorious. A legend. So I went looking for him. It wasn't easy because he keeps moving about the country all the time. But eventually, I tracked him down.

"I came straight out with it and asked him, 'How can I become a Christian?' Lok Bahadur explained I would need to ask Jesus to forgive my sins, and then invite Him to take charge of my life. I was thrilled. When I became a Christian that day, I felt I was in a different world. I moved from a world of fear of the gods, where I was trapped in a life I couldn't change, locked into my caste. And I moved into a world where fear and death are defeated and I've got the power to change myself and my circumstances. I had moved from one world to another. Suddenly, to that question, 'Are you happy?' I could answer, 'Yes'.

"At first, though I was very keen to change and to live like a Christian should, not a lot happened. I was trying to change myself on the inside while actually doing very little apart from going to church and learning the Bible. Then, one night, I had a dream. Jesus was in a very high place, looking down towards me and showing me His hands, torn by the nails, and telling me not to sleep but to work. When I woke up, I realised I wasn't doing anything for Him, just trying to take. I was taking from Him and from the church, but doing nothing and giving nothing back in return. That was my call to be a worker in the church, not just a member. Jesus wants working Christians, not sleeping Christians. The way I would change and grow on the inside was through my work. Sleepers stay as they are, workers change."

"You're quite right," I said, enthusiastically. "There are too many 'Consumer Christians' in Western churches and too few 'Disciples'. So what work did you start to do?"

"I started a small fellowship in my own village nearby. It's called Beldiah. I was the first Christian in the village. I work as a pastor during the day and, in the evening, I work as a tailor to earn enough money to live on. Tailoring is my caste profession. So now I really work!

"Of course, there was a lot of opposition. One evening there were sixteen of us having a service in our house when a great crowd of about five hundred gathered outside. They started to tear down the house with their bare hands and shouted that they were going to kill the Christians when they got to us. They thought we must be very rich because Western Christians would have given us money to bribe us. They wanted to find the money. It would have taken a long time, of course, because we were just as poor as they were. We were saved at the last moment by the local Congress Party leader who shouted at them that it was bad to attack people of other faiths at night. 'Persecute them in the daytime if you must!' he bellowed at them. Anyway, the crowd melted away and we prayed and prayed all night. The mob did not return next morning!

"Another time, an old lady who had become a Christian died. We buried her in the jungle with a Christian service. Later, 200 Hindus came round to my house to attack it again. They shouted at us, 'You are destroying our culture! And it's illegal!' The Hindus have very strongly held beliefs about burial rites, and we had defiled them. My wife and I stayed inside, terrified and praying fervently. Then the Chairman of the Village Development Committee stopped the mob. He told us to re-bury the lady quietly somewhere else that would stay a secret.

"When I went with half a dozen others to do this, the Christian ladies implored us, 'Don't go, they'll follow you into the jungle and kill you'. The mob had decided to follow us to the body and the women had found out. But I said, 'No, we must go and show we are not afraid of them. Satan must be defeated. We must have victory over Satan. Pray for us.' A big crowd did follow us and the mood was very ugly. But when we got to the grave, one of them said, 'Oh, let her rest, let it be'. He was suddenly deflated, and, when he said that, the rest of the crowd went the same way. They suddenly seemed sorry for how they were behaving and they melted away. So we left the lady to rest in peace and we had faced the enemy down.

"Now we have a church in Beldiah with fifty-five members. Most of them became Christians when they saw how we lived. We didn't want revenge on the people who pulled our house apart and nearly killed us. We showed no hatred, but neither did we give in to them. We never stopped giving out our tracts and preaching. Some who persecuted us were so impressed that they've become Christians themselves.

"So, now we're no longer persecuted, but we still have problems. This is a very poor area and there aren't many jobs. Many of the Christians have gone to India to find work. It's hard to keep in touch and it weakens the church. Also, we meet in a rented house but really need a proper church building. Problems don't end when persecution ends."

> In this world you will have trouble. But take heart!
> I have overcome the world.
>
> *John 16:33.*

CHAPTER 17

THE CHURCH GROWTH EXPERT

Prem Singh had walked for ten hours from his home village of Chainpur to get to Rajhar for a training course. He was seventy years old, a great age round here. His story flooded out unstoppably for a full half hour in the light of a single candle. I had no idea what was going on except that it was obviously dramatic. Eventually, my heroic interpreter managed to remember and retell the whole story:

"I stopped and stared. I became ravenously curious. What on earth was Sonderabad up to? There he was, standing in front of his house, surrounded by his buffalo and cows, his mouth working furiously, but no sound coming out of it, and his eyes were closed. Eventually, I could stand it no longer. 'Whatever are you doing, Sonderabad?' I shouted from the footpath. His mouth stopped working, his eyes opened and he looked round for the voice. 'My cow is sick', he said, 'and I'm praying for it.'

"I noticed that one of the cows was lying down and looked in a bad way. A sick cow is a major concern up in the hills where I live because our lives depend on the animals. 'Praying?' I asked, 'What is the meaning of 'praying'?' Sonderabad came over to me and explained. He produced a book about a man called Jesus who seemed to be God's son and who had great healing power.

"I was intrigued. I'd never been happy with the village witch doctor in Chainpur. We called him in to do the sacrifices for healing when someone was sick, but he was always so greedy for rice and money, and the sacrifices usually didn't work. Perhaps Sonderabad had found a better way to live. I was already fifty-four, not a bad age up in the hills, but I was still eager to learn. 'Can I have that sort of book?' I asked Sonderabad as I thumbed through his Bible. 'Well, they're very difficult to get hold of out here,' he replied, 'but next time I go in to Pokhara I'll get you one.'

"I got impatient. I didn't live in Sonderabad's village but I kept searching him out. 'Have you been to Pokhara and got me my book yet?' 'No, not yet'. I was getting desperate. I had to have the book that would tell me about this Jesus. Sonderabad was too slow and there were no other Christians in the area.

"Then, one day, walking along a path, I fell into conversation with a traveller. I told him how much I wanted a Bible. I was astonished at his reply. 'I'm a Christian, and I can give you a New Testament.' He fished in his bag and gave me one. At last! God had answered my prayer and I got very excited.

"I read it and re-read it several times from cover to cover. I noticed that the people who became Christians in the New Testament then got baptised. It's how they joined the church. So I decided I wanted to be baptised, too. But who could do it? I realised it would need a pastor, but I didn't know any, and there were no other Christians in Chainpur at all. There was only one pastor I had ever heard of. Everybody knew about him—such was by now the reputation of Lok Bahadur Tamang.

"So I set out on a journey to find Lok Bahadur. It wasn't easy because he keeps moving about the country all the time. But eventually I tracked him down and begged him to come to Chainpur with me and baptise me. So he came with me, and I was baptised, and now I felt I had joined the Christian church even though I was the only one for miles around.

"The trouble was that the village was scandalised. Old Prem Singh had adopted a Western religion. This was 1982 and it was against the law to change your religion. The village elders met to decide how to deal with me. They reported me to the District Police Station. After a while, the police came to my house and arrested me. At the police station, the policemen gathered round a large circular table, sitting on benches, and began a monumental drinking bout. Every so often, one of them, would come drunkenly over to me and beat me up. The binge lasted for three days and three nights, and for three days and three nights I was constantly beaten up, time after time after time. My body was just a mass of bruises, pulped. And my arms and legs were all useless. I couldn't even crawl, let alone walk.

"Then they let me go. They had taught me a lesson! After a few days, I was able to hobble slowly and painfully back home. The neighbours weren't exactly happy to see me. They thought I should have been locked away for a long time, but here I was, back after a few days, and still a

Christian. So they reported me again, this time to the City Police Office in Pokhara, hoping for proper action this time. I was arrested again, this time in a round-up of local Christians.

"But my wife followed me to the police station. She stayed arguing with the duty officer for hours. She wouldn't leave and she wouldn't shut up. Eventually, after a whole day of this, the officer let me go with a warning, just to get rid of her."

Then Jesus told his disciples a parable to show them that they should always pray and not give up. He said, 'In a certain town there was a judge who neither feared God nor cared about men. And there was a widow in that town who kept coming to him with the plea, 'Grant me justice against my adversary.' For some time he refused. But finally he said to himself, 'Even though I don't fear God or care about men, yet because this widow keeps bothering me, I will see that she gets justice, so that she won't eventually wear me out with her coming!'

And the Lord said, 'Listen to what the unjust judge says. And will not God bring about justice for his chosen ones, who cry out to him day and night? Will he keep putting them off? I tell you, he will see that they get justice, and quickly.'

Luke 18:1-8

"When we got back to Chainpur, the neighbours couldn't believe it. 'How does he do it? Each time he's arrested and we think we've got rid of him he comes back a few days later. It's useless, we might as well give up.' And give up they did, I'd won my freedom.

"But they didn't give up their interest in me, especially because I didn't show them any malice. 'Why don't you use the witch doctor any more, Prem Singh?' they asked. 'Because I've found a better way. I pray to Jesus and He heals us and drives away the demons,' I replied. Some of them noticed that my prayers seemed more effective than the witch doctor's rituals, and they asked me to teach them about Jesus.

"I acquired some Bibles and Christian tracts and passed them round the village. A small group said they would believe in Jesus the healer, and so a fellowship group started in my house where they learnt from my books.

"Every spare moment I had, I read my Bible and my Christian books. It was the only way I had of learning—Chainpur is pretty remote. But I did it out in the open, in the courtyard or on the balcony, where everybody could see me and get curious about what I was doing. 'What's Prem Singh up to now? What's so good about those books that he reads them all the time? There must be something good in them because he was ready to go to jail rather than give them up. Can we have a look at your books, Prem Singh?'

"So the neighbours who could read went through my books, and I explained things to those who didn't read or understand. Our small fellowship grew a little bigger.

"One night, as I slept at home, a commotion developed outside. Someone shook me wide awake. 'Come outside, some people have been bitten by the green snakes. They are going to die unless you pray for them.' I got up and went outside. The people had been brought right into my yard so there was no time to prepare and my whole credibility was on the line. If these people died then Jesus the healer was discredited in Chainpur. In the wilderness, the Israelites who had been bitten by snakes could be healed by going to the model snake erected on a pole. And Jesus had said:

Just as Moses lifted up the snake in the desert, so the Son of Man must be lifted up, that everyone who believes in him may have eternal life.

John 3:14,15

"In fear and trembling, I began to pray for them. 'Lord Jesus, heal these people and lift up your name in Chainpur.' Then we waited in suspense to see what would happen. Green snake bites were usually fatal, but the poison killed people fairly slowly. As we watched, the swellings and the other symptoms began to disappear. All of them recovered! So they all saw that Jesus was more powerful than the snakes and the witch doctor, and my church fellowship grew again.

"Later on, I was bitten on the foot myself by a green snake. First, I killed the snake. God had said to the snake in Genesis, 'He will crush your head and you will strike his heel.' (Gen. 3:15). Then I tied a cord tightly round my leg to stop the poison spreading and hobbled home to pray and wait. The neighbours came to watch, wondering if the gods were punishing me for being a Christian. The foot was agony, but I got better!

"The impact was just like on Malta in Acts chapter 28. A viper fastened itself on Paul's hand and he shook it off into the fire. The people all expected Paul to swell up and die because God was judging him. But when he came to no harm, they decided he had the power of God inside him. So it wasn't my body that swelled from the snake bite, it was my church fellowship!

"After this, they brought other sick people to me for healing. The sick were carried in, I laid my hands on them, prayed for them, and they walked out. I didn't ask for any money for this, like the witch doctor did. I just did it out of compassion and in faith. So the fellowship grew again.

"Now I've got 100% faith in God. He's real and He's powerful. By now I'm pastor of a congregation of 150. But although I'm seventy years old, and my wife has died, and I've been a Christian for sixteen years, I'm still learning. I've walked all this way through the hills to get some training. I still need to be trained and to bring back what I've learnt to share with the others."

Prem Singh had never heard of the concept of retirement. He will continue to grow his church in Chainpur on a remote hill in Nepal until his dying day. By that day, perhaps, the whole of the village which sent him to torture and jail will be calling him, 'Pastor'.

Jesus said to them, 'Go into all the world and preach the good news to all creation. Whoever believes and is baptised will be saved, but whoever does not believe will be condemned. And these signs will accompany those who believe: In my name they will drive out demons; they will speak in new tongues; they will pick up snakes with their hands; and when they drink deadly poison, it will not hurt them at all; they will place their hands on sick people, and they will get well.'

Mark 16:15-18

CHAPTER 18

ANOTHER ENOCH ?

"Enoch walked with God and he was not, for God took him"
Genesis 5:24 (RSV).

A group of us sat outside in the half-finished shell of an out-building that was to double up as a home for the Dil Bahadurs and a 'Sunday School' for the children. The group had met to discuss, once again, the extraordinary disappearance of Singha Bahadur. It happened in April, five months ago. The group was still agonising over whether there was any other possible explanation for what happened. Singha Bahadur's widow, or perhaps wife, was there, together with many of the men who were with him when he disappeared. The talk was serious and weighty with none of the laughing and joking which is usually irrepressible among Nepali Christians. At the end, they seemed to agree yet again that there was only one plausible explanation. Singha was another Enoch. Lok had already told me the story:

"Singha Bahadur was a witch doctor. He'd never had a haircut in his life and his hair was four feet long. He had magic symbols entwined in it. In February 1982 he had decided to become a Christian and he came with us on our annual prayer and fasting vigil at the top of the big hill."

At that moment the clouds parted and we could see the summit of the big hill from where we sat. It was bare and smooth, jutting out above all the others around, about 6000 feet above the low lying Terai.

"The church leaders go with me every year but this was Singha's first trip. During the week, the others all said to him, 'You can't keep your long hair and witch doctor tackle if you want to be a Christian. You've got to choose.' Singha knew what he had chosen and he asked them to cut his hair for him. 'No, no', they replied, 'it's against the law to cut off a witch doctor's hair. If you change your mind and complain, we'll be in trouble. If you really know the Lord, cut it off yourself. Now is the time for you to choose for yourself whether to be a Christian or not.'

"So Singha took a knife and cut his hair, so cutting himself off from his past. He buried his hair and his witch doctor amulets somewhere at the top of the hill. Fifteen days later we baptised him.

"So the prayer and fasting vigil became a highlight of Singha Bahadur's year. He was illiterate, but he kept asking questions and learning. He grew mainly as a man of prayer.

"As the years went on, Singha began to grow old and it became harder for him to struggle up the hill. Then, in 1995 and 1996, the prayer and fasting vigil lapsed. We were busy with other things. Singha was very sad about it and wondered if he'd ever climb the big hill again. But, this year, I said we must have a vigil again, it was too important to let go of.

"Singha's son was about to go to India to look for work, so Singha told him, 'This is our last meeting, so if you want to please God and walk with him, you need to read the book of Proverbs and live your life according to it.' So I think he had some sort of premonition. On 1st March, a few weeks before the vigil, at midday, Singha heard a voice calling out his name. 'Singha Bahadur! Pick up my cross and walk!' From that day onwards, he spent most of his time in prayer, sometimes all night, trying to obey the command to pick up the cross and walk with the cross bearer. All he wanted to do was to walk with God.

"As the week approached, the weather was cool and cloudy with a chance of thunderstorms. Some of the leaders said it was better not to go, but Singha was determined. 'No, we made a promise to God and we must keep it. This is the last time I'll be going to the hill, so I must go even if you don't.' So everyone went.

"It was the last Sunday in March, and I led a party of twenty-five on the fourteen hour walk to the summit of the big hill. Most of them were due to stay until Friday, though I had to leave early on Tuesday afternoon as I had some business elsewhere.

"It was cold and we had a hailstorm, but on the Monday morning we began the usual ritual. During the day we met together to pray and talk. We drank tea but only ate a bowl of rice if it was cold, to stop us getting ill. Otherwise we fasted. At night, we spread ourselves around the summit, each with enough space to pray out loud without disturbing the others too much. We Nepalis like praying out loud. Each evening we would decide what to pray about in the night, and in the morning we would compare notes. That was the way in which we tried to walk with God.

"On the Monday evening, Singha asked for prayer that his son would return quickly from India. Then he started lamenting that the Christians were all telling lies nowadays in the way they lived, just like everyone else. They weren't living holy lives, lives of truth, walking with God, they were untrustworthy, deceitful and corrupt. It was time to pray for this moral slide to stop, for the Christians to repent, be the salt of the earth again and walk with God.

"Next morning, Singha was the first to report on his night. He had had four dreams. One was about the Community Forest problem, one was about a family matter. The third was about the big bridge over the Kali Ghandaki. That was about Jesus being the bridge across the waters of death to eternal life. In the fourth, he saw himself being carried away floating on a peaceful white river. He was being carried powerfully away, but it was safe and it was peaceful. I said that we can't interpret that one just yet, but in a week or so we'll know the meaning of it.

"That afternoon I had to leave, but the others all told me what happened. Singha asked all the others, 'What exactly is "salvation"?' It was like a test question, and they tried different answers. Then they said, 'Are you asking because you do understand or because you don't understand?' 'I've been thinking deeply,' he replied, 'And I'm not sure I do understand.' So Dil Bahadur said, 'If you fall down a well, would you climb out by yourself or would you need help?' 'Help—someone else would have to pull me up on a rope.' 'That's right, someone else would need to save you from the well. Sin is the well that mankind has fallen into. Jesus is the rope come down from heaven to save us. God is the one who pulls us on the rope up to heaven. That's salvation—being plucked up to heaven when we're standing trapped in sin.' That seemed to satisfy him.

"They all settled down on Tuesday night as usual, and some of them could hear Singha praying away as usual until about midnight. Then he was quiet and they thought he must have dozed off. Next morning they were making the tea when they realised that Singha hadn't shown up, so they went over to his spot. It was just a few yards away, round the corner.

"All his things were there, including his hat and his shoes, but there was no sign of him or the clothes he'd been wearing. He'd been in a gap in the rocks with some thatching grass laid over the top to create a sort of makeshift tent. There was a gap in the thatching grass above where he'd been sleeping, big enough for a man to go through. The broken strands were all pointing upwards as though something heavy had shot through them from below.

"They searched for him all day, but found no sign whatsoever. If he'd wandered off they would have found footprints or some sort of sign. He would have been barefoot—they still had his shoes. We kept looking for him for a month. We mounted expeditions to search for him, we took binoculars and other gear to search. We went to the foot of every steep hill in the area to see if he had fallen off something. We had prayer meetings for him. We cared for and comforted his family. But we have never found the slightest sign of him.

"His son came back from India soon afterwards and told us he had had a dream about his father, on or about the night he disappeared. His father was standing on a hill with five great rocks sticking out of the ground near the summit. He was standing in a particular place between the rocks when he shot upwards into a cloud and the cloud carried him away.

"We took his son up the hill to have a look. He'd never been there before. When he arrived, he got very excited. 'This is it, this is the hill I saw in my dream, there are the five rocks!' We showed him where his father had been. 'That's it, that's the place he was standing in!' His son isn't a Christian but he went down the hill rejoicing. He was convinced that God had taken his father and spared him the experience of death.

"Some high caste Hindus, who are enemies of mine, tried to persuade Singha's family to prosecute me for murder. But his son said, 'No, he wasn't murdered, God took him. He told me to read the book of Proverbs. Stop your mischief and go and read it yourselves!' That shut them up. Anyway, I had left on the Tuesday afternoon. I'm in the clear, but the others who were with Singha have still got a problem. They haven't reported it officially to the police yet because they might get charged. But until it's reported his son can't inherit his land. It's a tricky situation.

"Anyway, his Hindu neighbours all say he was a good man and it is no surprise if his Jesus has taken him. They've no sense of anything amiss.

"The night before Singha left, he said to his wife, 'I want to ask you something. It's the last chance I have to ask you this. What is the most important thing to you? What would you most like to have in the future?' She answered him, 'Now I'm getting on a bit I'd like enough money to keep me comfortable and pay someone to help me with the farm.' Singha replied, 'Then wherever you go, you'll live in darkness because you wanted money and security rather than the Lord.' That was the last thing he ever said to her. But she's with us now and she's happy that the Lord took him, and I don't think she'll be in darkness for ever."

It was a joy for me to talk to Singha's wife that afternoon with the group. It felt like an excellent bereavement therapy session. It was a privilege to express my feelings for her, and catch the light of a dawning new hope in her eyes.

Enoch walked with God after the birth of Methuselah three hundred years and had other sons and daughters. Thus all the days of Enoch were three hundred and sixty five years. Enoch walked with God, and he was not, for God took him.

Genesis 5:22-24

CHAPTER 19

CREDENTIALS

The sun broke through the clouds, and, by mid afternoon, it was painfully hot. I packed my rucksack and the three of us set off for Barataidi. Lok led the way across the flat rice paddy fields and the interpreter and I followed in single file. We had to watch our step on the narrow, slippery pathway between the fields. When we came to ford a river, the other two just waded through in their flip flops like everyone else. I had to take off my walking boots and socks and carry them. It was quite a performance and I drew a small crowd. After a mile of this, we came to the foot of the hill. Geographically, this was a significant point. We had reached the absolute northern extremity of the North Indian Plain which stretched almost forever to the south. To the north lay the hills of middle Nepal, the Himalayas and high Tibet. We started climbing through the jungle on a well-worn track, slippery after the rain and steaming in the sun.

At first the climb was quite steep, then it levelled out into a gentler incline. I could see ahead of me a large shelf of land, sloping gradually up to the hills behind, mostly wooded but with some clearings. As we climbed, I looked back and saw the giant river's flood plain shining with reflected sun down on the Terai. It was snaking its way through the Chitwan National Park where the tourists go to photograph tigers and rhino and to ride elephants. But no tourists walked this path and I drew the usual inquisitive stares as we reached the lower edge of Barataidi.

At first, we walked through the eighty houses of the people without land papers who were being threatened with eviction. Children gathered round, everyone we passed greeted Lok and he had a few words with them. Everyone was so friendly, it was hard to imagine the various battles of Barataidi all happening on this spot. Lok took us off the track to have a look at the flimsy school building that had been put up with international help. The crowd of followers grew, all demanding their photographs. Some of the children were suffering from worms and malnutrition, and their clothes were in tatters.

Then we reached a smaller area of more substantial houses, turned left through the hedge, and there was Lok Bahadur's house. Phulmaya had walked back earlier, and now she greeted us warmly. They showed us round. Everything was made of timber, taken from the Community Forest which started a few yards up the hill. Arranged around the courtyard was the main house, with a balcony and sleeping quarters above. There was electricity down by the main road in Rajhar, but not up here. The rhythms of life here were still dictated by the sun. Below was mainly storage space, with benches and stools for sitting on just outside under the balcony. Next to the main building was a smaller one which acted as kitchen-diner. The floor level wood burning stove was at one end, and a dining table at the other. Outside, next to the dining room building, was a table with water jars. This was the washing and washing-up area. Behind it was an outside, Asian style, toilet, clean and well-kept. No smells. Then there was a range of hen huts, rabbit hutches, a kennel for the dog, pigeon houses and small barns containing goats and buffalo. The pet parrot, in its basket, hung down from the balcony. Behind the washing-up area was a vegetable plot, and the other side of the track was a rice paddy field. This was Lok and Phulmaya's smallholding.

It looked and felt exactly like I imagined a medieval subsistence farm in England would have been, a living history lesson to a modern Westerner. A lot of money for many different projects had passed through Lok's hands over the years. He is a national figure and church leader. He is authorised to anoint pastors and appoint them to churches. Many churches consider him as their overall leader. He acts like a bishop. And yet, most of his living is earned by vigorous and skilful subsistence farming. Some bishops live in palaces. Lok lives in a wooden house built by his own hands deep in the jungle, his integrity impregnable.

The interpreter and I were given the two best beds, side by side, in a room upstairs. While daylight lasted, I sorted out my sleeping bag and arranged the mosquito net. Lok had disappeared to see a few people. Phulmaya invited us into the dining room and Lok re-appeared from somewhere. I was offered the seat of honour—a fine-looking hardwood chair with a high back and arms. My thin, spindly frame measures ten stone and five foot ten inches with no padding on my rear end. I tried to sit in the chair and stuck fast between the arms. We all had a good laugh as I wriggled free, and I realised afresh how very thin the average Nepali is. Everyone piled into mountains of *dhal bhat*. I asked for a half-portion, ate half of that and felt as full as after Christmas dinner. How do they eat like that and stay so thin?

We sat on our beds by the light of a candle and talked to Lok before bedtime. "How many churches look to you for leadership?"

"By 1995 there were sixty-five altogether, forty-five here in Nawalparaisi and twenty up in Dhading. Either directly or indirectly, I was responsible for starting almost all of them. But also I'm Western Region Chairman of the National Churches Fellowship of Nepal (NCFN). It used to be called the Nepal Christian Fellowship (NCF). So there are lots of other churches I have to go and visit. To have sixty-five churches of your own, though, is overwhelming. It's really too many to cope with. A few years ago, I was able to send thirty-eight pastors and trainee pastors to Bible School, some in Kathmandu, some in Darjeeling, and some in America. This fulfilled part of the Isaiah chapter 61 prophecy—'You will be named ministers of our God. You will feed on the wealth of nations.'

"I was able to find money for salaries but not for buildings and all my churches were still poor. After the Revolution in 1990, the foreign denominations had freedom to come into Nepal, and they have brought money with them. Some churches have gone over to them, but that's transfer growth, not real growth. When they offer money for church buildings, they demand their name on the door, and the church then has to join their denomination and come under their control. Two years ago, most of my churches left me to join these other groups. I understood why. I didn't have the resources to keep them all going, and I'm not interested in empire building. So I anointed twelve pastors for them and sent them out with my blessing. We keep on good terms. But now I'm left with only ten churches in Nawalparaisi and one in Dhading, which we'll go and see next week. All my ten Tharu churches left together and formed a group called 'Friendship Church'. You and I would have been guests of honour at a new one this afternoon if the rain hadn't swollen the river and cut us off from them.

"It can leave me with a heavy heart when my churches move on because I worry it was for the wrong motive. I built the people, the outside groups built the buildings, and so they take the people. It's the wrong way round. The groups with money should build the buildings and let the people decide who to relate to. But, of course, I have to accept it and let them go with my blessing. The worst thing is attitudes to money. At heart they left for financial reasons and decided to go and chase money. Now they've got materialistic aims, spiritually they are worse off. Financial things don't satisfy. And some pastors fall into the trap of building their own empires and nurturing jealousies, competing with each other. I think in the end, all the well-supported churches will die, at least spiritually and, perhaps, numerically. The self-supporting ones will carry on and grow. You can't serve two masters—God and money. Some churches chase money and others serve God.

"Some of the pastors and churches are seeing this now. They feel they've lost out spiritually, and they don't like being ordered about by denominations. Two churches in Nawalparaisi and five in Dhading have just asked me to take them back and be their overseer. They'll also return to NCF. I think there will be more. It's hard to know what will happen in the future, but the political situation is getting worse and there may be new persecution in the next two or three years. The church nationally is growing so fast it may need a sifting out to sort the wheat from the chaff and become pure again."

I asked Lok about evangelism. "What sort of strategy do you have nowadays?"

"I've never been to college and read up on strategies so I don't suppose I know how to have one! But what we usually do is look for one individual new Christian, probably who lives in an area without any Christians so far. Perhaps they met the Lord when they were healed. Then we disciple them in Christian living. We teach them, we love them, we make them strong. They learn Christian beliefs, and we help them talk about their faith with others, but the most important thing is to help them change their lives. These days in Nepal we are getting professional preachers and expert evangelists who sell their books for profit and ask large fees. They're getting rich. You've heard of 'Rice Christians'. Some of these are 'Buffalo Christians'! They may know the right things and say the right things, but they don't live the right way and their converts are few and flimsy.

"This is the point—we read the Bible but unbelievers read us like a book. They watch us and they're not stupid. If we just live like everybody else we'll attract no one. If we can strengthen one key person in a place to live as a Christian should with the fruits of the Spirit, then they have the spiritual power to attract others. A new church will be planted. I don't know if it's a strategy but that's what we do, and it works.

"A while ago, there was a month long discipleship course. It was a mix of book learning and street evangelism. I think it was a good course. There were certificates and qualifications at the end of it. Some of them got great marks in the exams, but no converts on the streets. I sent an illiterate Magar from Nawalparaisi on the course. He makes earthenware pots. He found a similar family on the street during the course, making their pots, and he witnessed to them. They became Christians and then they brought others to the Lord. But my Magar couldn't do the course work and he couldn't even take the exam because he was illiterate. So to whom do we give first place on the course?

"But sometimes I do feel it these days when the younger pastors have all their qualifications and education. Sometimes the city types laugh at me at conferences when the country bumpkin shovels in the seconds of *dhal bhat*. But I'm genuinely hungry and need to take the opportunity to fill up!"

Lok laughed. There was no bitterness in all this, just a wry humour at the situation.

"The education is wonderful! I wish I had been educated like that. I get as many of my people as possible on to courses and into colleges. I've got no training and qualifications like they have. My training is being hauled before the village *panchayat* eight times, to the police station twice, to the court twice, to be beaten and robbed and threatened and spat on and to come back for more. Those are my credentials and that's my training!"

CHAPTER 20

FUTURE HOPE

I felt so full after the egg noodles for breakfast I announced I would fast for the rest of the day. Lok went off to run the village meeting about the Forest accounts, so I strolled off in the early morning sun up the hill into the forest. It was in superb condition and obviously well-managed. Every so often, shapes would appear, rustling in the undergrowth or walking along the path. On the outside were leaves and twigs and branches, fodder hacked off bushes and trees to feed the goats. The outside usually hid the inside completely. But, if you looked carefully, you could just make out that the inside consisted of a small child. School was a luxury many of them could not afford—their job was to feed the animals and so help feed the family. They reminded me of the blind man from Bethsaida whom Jesus had healed.

> Jesus asked, 'Do you see anything?' He looked up and said, 'I see people; they look like trees walking around.'
>
> *Mark 8:24*

I got back and started chatting to Moses. Moses was Lok and Phulmaya's youngest child, and the only one still at home. He was nineteen. The other two sons and two daughters were all married, and there were seven grandchildren so far. As I looked round the farm there were four objects invading from the modern world—a guitar, a mountain bike and two football boots. All four belonged to Moses. He and his friend were about to go down to the main road to find a television set. Nepal were playing India at football and there was much to discuss about prospects. They both played for the local team—Rajhar—and there was a match this tea-time. I asked Moses if he had heard of Sheffield Wednesday and was downcast when he hadn't. So I asked him if he had heard of Manchester United and was thrilled at the blankness of his stare. Moses favoured Western-style clothes and his ambition was to get a job in Kathmandu, or, even better, abroad. Lok's own roots were firmly in the traditional soil of Nepal, but the West was drawing the next generation to new ways.

Then I settled down on the benches outside the house to talk to Phulmaya, who had been busy as usual, working the farm and the kitchen while Lok was out at the meeting. I wanted to know how she felt when Lok got taken to police stations and fell into trouble.

"I stay at home and pray for the Lord to deliver him. I'm not worried how I'd cope without him because I do most of the work round here anyway." She laughed. "He's out most of the time as it is. I'm a traditional Nepali woman. I sacrifice my own comforts for the family. I never really consider how I'm feeling myself, I just get on with the job of supporting my husband and trusting God for him. We do share things and talk them through and laugh a lot about life together. But he never tells me the really bad things!"

I asked Phulmaya about how she got married, and she laughed again and retold the tale. "My father's still alive in Dhading. I've been back several times over the years and I still respect his wisdom!"

Child mortality in Nepal is one of the highest in the world, and hardly a family in the country is free of its trauma. People in the West may imagine that losing a child in a culture where it is so common can't be quite so devastating for parents. I asked Phulmaya, "Could you tell me about Rajina and whether being a Christian made any difference to the way you coped with losing her?"

"She became very ill and we got her into Tansen Hospital. She got better there and came home again. She was well for another eighteen months before she fell ill again. Lok took her into Tansen Hospital again and left her there. As soon as he arrived back home, I went to stay with her. By the time I got there, she had died. She was fourteen. Our friend, a nurse from Norway, gave me a lot of love and help, and the Church in Tansen gave me great support. That's one difference being a Christian made.

"But when I saw her in the coffin, I just broke down and cried and cried and cried. My friend kept telling me God would help me and she was so encouraging. But for months I just cried and yearned for Rajina. Once or twice I thought I heard her voice calling my name, and tried to look for her.

"Then one night I had a dream. It was more vivid than a normal dream—it was real. I could see Rajina, and she was washing her hair. She looked up and said to me, 'I've heard you crying so bitterly for me, now I've come to tell you not to cry. There's no need. I'm in heaven with Jesus.' From then on I stopped crying every day and began to come to terms with it."

"Yes, that's the most important difference," I replied, "we still have our grief but we also have our hope. We lost our son, Matthew, when he was ten and so we've been through the same things as you. It's a bond I feel between us and so many Nepali parents." I gave Phulmaya a copy of 'Matthew', the book I had written about our bereavement and the difference being a Christian made. Their eldest son spoke English, so they would give it to him to read. "It seems a strange thing," I said, "that God would heal so many people through you and Lok, yet take your own daughter. But she's in heaven and one day you'll see her again and hug her, and have her for ever, and all will be well."

We each shed a tear, Phulmaya went back to the kitchen, and I went hunting butterflies with the zoom lens. Soon, Lok returned with the accountant, all smiles. The accountant, in high spirits, showed me the accounts with ticks in red ink all over them and his signature underneath. "Very good accounts!" was all the English I got out of him. Lok said the village meeting had gone well, and the two of them disappeared into the diner for *dhal bhat*. The interpreter said to me, "Do you realise that accountant is a Brahmin, and he's gone in to eat with a Tamang Christian in the Tamang's own home? Brahmins would normally consider someone like Lok virtually untouchable. That's wonderful, he must think a great deal of Lok—it's a real sign of hope that the caste barriers are breaking down round here."

It was now 11.30am and I felt like a siesta. But Phulmaya summoned me into the diner for *dhal bhat*. I was still full with egg noodles, but did my pathetic best to be polite and cram in some rice on top! We were due at the Dil Bahadurs' this evening, and I implored the interpreter to explain I couldn't possibly eat with them as well. He told me they wouldn't understand and I'd just have to take my chance.

After siesta, we got ready to walk down the hill to Rajhar. Another night on the concrete beckoned before an early bus to Pokhara. We sat a while in the shade, waiting for the sun to slip a little further down the clear blue sky, when Phulmaya pulled us into the diner again. "Just a bowl of egg noodles to keep you going till this evening".

After fond farewells, we retraced our steps to the church. Dil Bahadur welcomed us and went off to find a hen for tea. I went exploring Rajhar. There seemed to be a lot of noise coming from one direction and quite a crowd gathering. I followed the noise and found a huge football field with a match in progress. There was a crowd of many hundreds watching Moses and his friends do their stuff. It wasn't like football in England because most people seemed to be just enjoying the atmosphere and chatting to their friends. Half the crowd ignored the football for a while to stare at me. Eventually, someone shouted it was rude for so many people to stare quite so obviously even if this freak did have red hair. After that, they went back to the game. When the visitors scored, everybody cheered and looked happy about it. Football was so new round here they seemed to be enjoying it for its own sake. Progress, doubtless, and Manchester United, will catch up with them one day and they will learn to hate opponents like civilised people do.

Dil Bahadur's wife firmly believed I had been starving for the last two days up in Barataidi, and things needed putting right. The children looked at me pityingly as they shovelled in the rice, and I struggled to eat a few scraps. "Is he ill?" they were asking each other. The main thing in favour of my night's sleep was that it was brief. Moses met me and put me on the right bus in Narayanghat for Pokhara. Lok went to the District Office with the accounts and the next round of his legal battle for the Community Forest.

We would meet up again in a few days in Mugling, ready for a trip to Dhading, up into the hills of Lok's birth, the heartland of the Tamangs, and the very edge of the white Himalayas. This promised to be a great and dangerous adventure.

CHAPTER 21

ONLY ONE GOD

There is nothing more reassuring to an Englishman travelling in foreign parts than a Land Rover. It pulled into the compound at 7am looking tough and businesslike. I tried to look the same. We loaded my gear on board and were joined by a young man called Shoba, who was to be my porter, and a friend of the driver who fancied a day out. All we had to do now was collect my interpreter for the trip, Pradeep. Pradeep lived in town behind his shop which sold clothes and bags and batiks to the tourists. Unfortunately, as I spoke no Nepali and my three new friends spoke no English, it was not easy to explain to the driver where to go first. At last, we waylaid a lady who spoke some English to translate for me.

Pradeep's wife and two pretty daughters were there at the shop to wave us off. The older daughter had been born with a constantly weeping right eye, and for three months no eye specialist or ointment was able to clear it up. It seemed serious enough to threaten the sight of the eye. Pradeep had read parts of the Bible in the past and he knew one or two Christians, though he was still a nominal Hindu. Then he decided he really needed to find out if God existed.

"I complained to whatever God there might be, 'Why me? Why my child? If you're there at all I need you now!' While I was thinking this, I saw a couple of American tourists standing in the road, looking up at the mountains. I thought to myself, 'These people have spent a lot of money to come here and look at our wonderful part of creation, I ought to be friendly to them.' So we got chatting. Then my wife brought our daughter out, and they said, 'Oh, she's crying, what's the matter?' I explained that she had this eye problem and none of the doctors could help.

"Then they asked something that surprised me—'We've been talking about creation, do you believe in the Creator?' I said, 'I'm not sure, but there must be someone who made these mountains and forests and this lake.' 'We think that if we pray for your daughter, the creator God will hear us and heal her. Would you let us do that?' they asked. 'Okay,' I said, 'come into the shop.' They prayed for her and we put her to bed for the night.

"The next morning we got ready to clean the eye out and open it up carefully, but when we went to her we didn't need to—it was completely healed! We were absolutely amazed. 'Their God, their Jesus, He must have healed her,' we shouted. Then I reasoned—'The Americans said there was only one God so he must be God of Nepal as well as America, so why can't the same God be my God as well as theirs?'

"So I read the Bible from Genesis to Revelation, and it was wonderful, and I got baptised at Ram Ghat church, and so did my wife. Then the man next door got ill. The local astrologer said he'd been got at by the Demon of the Lake so he should sacrifice a chicken at sunset. But I told him about our daughter and offered to pray with him. Next evening he dragged himself round, he was so slow and weak, and he couldn't eat at all! We prayed with him and he crawled away. Next morning, I opened up our front door and there he was outside, running in the street. And that day he ate like a Nepali—a mountain of rice as high as Machhapuchhare! And lots of other people I've prayed for have been healed."

With Pradeep on board, the Land Rover set out on the main road out of Pokhara in the direction of Kathmandu. We were heading for the junction town of Mugling, where the road from the Terai snakes in from Narayanghat through a spectacular gorge. Lok would meet us there. At first the road goes straight and level through fringe townships and villages, and then it climbs to a watershed through mile after mile of paddy fields littered with people in broad-brimmed straw hats operating sluice systems and shoring up mud banks to keep the precious, growing rice well-watered. Being the monsoon season, clouds obscured the higher hills and the mountains. Then we hit a shower. Suddenly, we were in a proper monsoon and it was like driving through a waterfall. I thought, "If I get caught out of doors in one of these, all my notes for this book will be wet pulp."

But, by Mugling, the clouds had lifted and the sun had come out. Mugling was a string of tea shops and *dhal bhat* 'Fast Food' cafes catering for an endless supply of buses making their way through the wooded hills clustering around. It was an island of human squalor in a sea of natural splendour.

The problem with the sunshine was Pradeep. He explained it to me: "In heat and bright light I get migraines.

If it stays cloudy and I wear my sunglasses and use my umbrella and pray hard I might be okay. But I can't carry any luggage. I can only come if a porter carries my rucksack." I agreed to this with a bright smile and a heavy heart. If Shoba carried Pradeep's gear, he could take very little of mine. It looked like I was going to be porting a heavy rucksack just like Shoba.

We hung around Mugling, keeping an eye on the buses, getting steadily more anxious about Lok. I suggested the others eat their *dhal bhats* now, but they said it was only polite to wait for Lok and eat with him. He was always particular about his *dhal bhat* at Mugling. I ate my Snickers and drank my Fanta anyway. Leaving the shade, I wandered up the street under the hot sun looking for my man, surrounded by sellers of fruit, nuts, snacks, poppadums and fish, all offering me great deals, and by beggars offering me great, sad eyes. Suddenly he appeared out of the heat and exhaust fume haze, striding confidently towards me, moving twice as fast as anyone else, smiling and waving. "I saw the Land Rover and thought it would be you. So I ate my *dhal bhat* straight away so as not to hold you up when we met." The others groaned. I manfully refrained from saying, 'I told you so', and they ordered and ate while Lok and I watched on. We were two of a kind, inexperienced observers of other people's feasts, and twitchy from inaction.

The main road to Kathmandu had recently been rebuilt and we sped along it until we came to the junction of the track to Dhading Town. It started with a spectacular bridge over the Trisuli River, and then mile upon mile of rough, tough track along which the Land Rover bounced, finally in its true element.

"Nothing less than a Land Rover could tackle this track," I thought to myself as I crashed around in the back. We rounded a bend, and there in front of us was a single-decker bus, so tightly packed with people they were spilling out of the doors and squeezing out of the windows. It wasn't going much slower than us, and it looked like it would break into pieces as it barged, banged and bounced along the track. But Tata make their buses brutally rough and tough down in Jamshedpur. It came to no more harm than its battered exterior could absorb. Still, better to lurch in a Land Rover than bounce in a bus. Unfortunately, the truth of this was only brought home to me on the return trip when a giant rut at high speed catapulted me off the back seat of the bus and concussed my head on the roof.

We were dropped off in the heat and dust of Main Street, Dhading Town. It was like a set from a 'Western'—a one street town set crudely down on the dusty trail at the edge of the wild frontier. Rough customers swaggered down Main Street in wicked stubble seeking hotels featuring tin baths. You have heard of 'Spaghetti Westerns': If they ever make a '*Dhal bhat* Western', then Dhading is the place. I moseyed into a bar and ordered in my best mean gravel voice. "Four Cokes, barman, and make it fast." I reached down to check my 'Thirty-Six Shooter', strapped to my right hip. When it came to snapping the natives, I was the quickest draw in the East with my Canon 50E. But were there any natives who would want to snap at me?

As Lok talked about the impact of healings on these remote communities, I recalled a recent incident. The four-year-old daughter of a prominent family in one of the Tamang hill villages was sick, and soon to die. All the village did sacrifices and incantations for her, but nothing worked. A teenage boy in the village had been down to

Raxaul, and, while he was there, had casually picked up a Christian tract. It was about healing, and had a picture of the cross on the front. It said that, if people prayed in the name of Jesus, a person may be healed. He kept it under his sleeping mat and forgot about it.

But now the boy remembered the tract and took it to the village elders. They asked the girl's father, "Should we try praying to this God as the others don't seem to work?" So they went to their temple and prayed to Jesus. Instantly, the dying girl got better. The whole village was so impressed, they all decided to become Christians, and Jesus became their village god. They made a cross and put it in their temple, even though they didn't really know what it signified.

For months afterwards, all the sick were prayed for in the name of Jesus and all of them got better. Then a touring evangelist arrived at another village in the area, hoping to start a church somewhere. "There's already a Christian village near here, over on that hill over there," said the villagers. "Oh no there isn't," said the evangelist, "That's why I'm here—we've never had contacts with that village." "Oh yes there is," repeated the villagers. "Oh no there isn't", insisted the evangelist. "There can't be because no Christians have ever come to evangelise the area". "Oh yes there is," they insisted. "Go and see!"

So the evangelist went, and found the Christian village which had never had any contact with the outside Christian world at all. He taught them about the whole of the Christian Gospel. As soon as he did this, the automatic healings stopped, and successful prayer for healing became spasmodic.

"Yes, churches have been starting like that all over the area in the last few years," said Lok, "Twenty of them looked to me for leadership and belonged to the Nepal Church Fellowship. But then, after the Revolution in 1990 and the churches had freedom, the denominations started moving in, with more money and resources than we could offer. So 'Gospel For Asia' has taken most of the twenty, though I'm still on good terms with them all. I only look after one directly now, and that's the one we're going to see. It's in a village called Bhirchet at the top of a hill not far from Kapure where I was born. It's a day and a half to walk from here. The other churches are three or four days walk so we haven't time for them on this trip."

Just then, an old man wandered by and greeted Shoba warmly. It turned out he was from Shoba's village and he was a Christian. So I asked him why he was a Christian. "For my own benefit," he replied. "I don't have to do any of those expensive sacrifices to the spirits, and don't have to give expensive food to the monks and the witch doctors. It's a much cheaper religion. All we have to do when we're ill is to pray and we get better. It's great. Everyone in our village is a Christian now and we've got three churches." He was certainly enthusiastic and had clearly grasped the wonderful truth of the free grace of God, and the gift of Jesus to be the one perfect sacrifice for all people and all time. But he didn't seem to have much concept of what was expected of him in return—to live a new life, to love his neighbour and to share his faith.

"You see, they've all become Christians so fast and there are so few of us to teach them. Some of them need a lot of teaching," lamented Lok, in near despair. "I know," I sympathised, " We've got lots of Christians obsessed with what they can get out of God rather than what they can give to Him!"

Lok decided it was time to move. The sun had slipped down the sky part way, but it still seemed pretty powerful to me. I wondered how Pradeep would cope. "Badly," was the answer. The hill was steep, the humidity was high and the sun was on our backs. Pradeep suffered every step of the way. He was suffering physically, but he was also suffering emotionally. "I'm so sorry. You should have brought an interpreter who could walk, I should never have come," he lamented. But most of the time he just mumbled, "Why, Lord, why?" The Lord did not answer him at the time, although he did two days later.

Finally, Pradeep collapsed in the shade and Lok decided to abandon him. I followed Lok as he strode impatiently up the hill, while Shoba stayed with Pradeep to try and prod him to the top in due course. After another hour or two of climbing, we came upon a small hamlet with a lodge, and Lok indicated we should stay the night. They had Coca Cola and Fanta bottles, so this seemed okay to me. As the sun started setting, turning grey clouds ginger and green hills grey, two figures slid slowly into view. I clapped and cheered, while Shoba's shining incisors grinned out of the gloaming. Pradeep made wordlessly for the pitch dark upper room of the rustic lodge and collapsed on the inner-most bed.

As *dhal bhat* began to cook on the wood fire, I enjoyed the orange sunset followed by the pure white stars. The sky was clear and the moon was down. The heavens quickly filled with the myriad pin point lights of the brighter, nearer suns. Gradually, the fuzzier clouds of the Milky Way and the distant galaxies emerged from the gathering gloom. A shooting star blazed a trail out of this eternity into the world of men, dying as it shone, like a parable of the Saviour from heaven. During the day, my gaze enraptured by the massive hills and awe inspiring mountains beyond, I rejoiced in the supreme Creator who had manufactured this greatest scenery on God's earth. Now the Himalayas disappeared, suddenly insignificant compared with the galaxies. Surely they, not a few pinpricks on the face of one small planet, were the best measure for human eyes of the enormity of the creator God.

Our host pumped up the tilly lamp. A different Pradeep reappeared, mended by the blessed dark. Galaxies of *dhal bhat* appeared for me to push around the plate with my 'special guest fork' while the others conveyed it to their mouths with their right hands.

Pradeep favoured an early night so we could walk in the cool dark of the wee small hours. The four of us clambered the rickety steps to find what rest we could before the big day ahead.

The rats kept me alert most of the night, though the thunderstorm was an added stimulation. Up in the roof space of the crude lodge, the smoke from the fire which cooked last night's *dhal bhat* lingered in the trapped air. The roof was slated with good six inch square grey slates, about two feet above my head as I lay stretched out on the bed. This was solid wood and as hard as your dining table. My head was lodged against the front wall of the little house, and my feet pressed firmly against the back wall. So I was about an inch taller than the house was wide. But the rats were the main problem, up above somewhere, scrabbling noisily, and bringing down heaps of roof debris and droppings on to my rucksack and walking socks. When, I fretted, would a rat be falling on my face? At length, I reached out in the pitch dark to check my alarm clock and grabbed something warm and fleshy. I screamed and threw it away. It was Pradeep's foot.

The clock said 4am. Pradeep said, "Let's wake Lok and Shoba and start walking while it's cool. I don't want another migraine like yesterday." Doing no good in the bed, I readily agreed, and we kicked the others awake. Breakfast was glucose biscuits and Coke, though Pradeep had another of my *Dioralytes,* fancying it as a migraine cure.

We walked up a good track, with a half moon for illumination. The great hills of Dhading were mysterious silhouettes carved out by the moonlight. I had thought we finished climbing yesterday, but, as usual, I was completely wrong. The track wound up and up for another hour or more, then along a great ridge as dawn steadily revealed the matchless scale of the scenery. The great snow peaks of the Ganesh Himal stood high and proud behind the deep ranks of hills guarding them. These rose ten thousand feet or more, but they were mere new born chicks under the wing of the Himalayan mother hen.

Cumulus was forming rapidly, but, unfortunately, well below us in the valleys. The thin cirrus above succumbed to the enthusiastic rays of the morning sun. In the dying weeks of the monsoon, the air was hopelessly soaked. Even at dawn, my clothes were as wet as in the washing machine. I was walking through a giant sauna, and someone kept turning up the controls. Other people wrote about growing churches in lounge suit London and comfortable California. Why had I picked on Bhirchet?

After an easy stretch through jungle, we stopped at 6.30 for second breakfast—egg noodles made up on a wood fire in a thatched hut. I made friends with a hen clucking at my feet. I warned it sternly never to be the last one into the hutch of an the evening. This was the precise mistake made by last night's dinner. Instead of topping the roost, she had topped the *dhal bhat*.

Now the path lay steeply down through terraced paddy fields of tall, green rice with swelling grains from the plenteous monsoon. We rounded a bend and a walker coming the other way greeted Lok warmly. It was his brother-in-law. "We came here once," said, Lok, a memory triggered, "With a team of ten and 6,000 tracts to give out. We handed them all out and I think many people became Christians. Tracts work very well here. Christianity is new and they've no prejudices against it. If a tract explains to people that God loves them and will answer their prayers through Jesus, they will try it out and find it works!

"Another time, I think it was in 1980, I was round here, preaching with Kali Bahadur, and we had a big crowd of people at a meeting. There was a lady in the kitchen, preparing food for everyone. Suddenly, she fell to the ground, white foam started coming out of her mouth, and she couldn't speak. Nothing like that had ever happened to her before. She seemed to have been attacked by an evil spirit. We hit her gently on the forehead with a Bible and I said to her, 'Satan speak now, tell me your name.' The woman answered, but in a very strange voice, 'I live in the jungle and I live in the trees and by the rivers and on the resting places by the roads. I go from resting place to resting place, from hill to hill.' So I asked, 'Why have you come here you evil spirit?' And she replied, 'I thought you might give me something to eat, but, if you don't, I might as well go!' Then the whole crowd of us felt a cold breeze as the spirit seemed to come out of the lady, leave the kitchen, go out of the building and into the chicken run. The lady was fine after that, but the chickens all ran around confused and agitated, and extremely noisy. They all made an extraordinary 'Kirrrooo Kirrrooo' sort of sound."

Lok did a fine imitation of the well remembered noise, and we all had a go at it for a few hilarious minutes. "So it was like 'Legion' and the spirits Jesus sent into the pigs," I concluded. In Dhading, we were living in Bible times. I had stepped into the pages and culture of Scripture. It was coming alive in front of my wide eyes.

At eight, we stopped again when Shoba found some friends in a shack by the path. Lok Bahadur took the chance to have a third breakfast—potato, corn and beans with chunks of chilli. I asked a man carrying bananas if he would sell me two, but he refused, saying they were for a festival. However, an opportunistic small boy immediately arrived with two bananas and said, "Five rupees". I proffered a new, red Rs5 note and he went off grinning broadly at the white mug who paid 5p for only two bananas. He returned straight away with two more bananas and received another red note.

As we walked in the growing heat, a glorious variety of huge and colourful butterflies flattered to deceive, flying off the moment the macro lens finally focused. However, I did catch one asleep and another one dead so I may yet be able to show off my wild butterfly photo album. The wild flowers were equally gorgeous, with the added advantage of being unable to fly off at the crucial moment.

The path sank steeply into the valley floor of the great Anku Khola. Near the bottom, we crossed a tributary on a long and decrepit example of Nepal's "Never look down but know which planks to avoid" two foot wide suspension bridges. It is possible to get sea sick on these bridges as they buck and sway under the weight of travellers. But if, while on a bridge, you see a donkey train embarking in the opposite direction, turn round and run! Who cares about dignity?

We scrambled down to the monsoon—swollen torrent and took off nearly all our clothes. Pradeep had spent the dawn hours singing and praising the Lord who had delivered him from yesterday's migraine. But in the growing morning heat a new one was forming, so he repeatedly baptised himself by total immersion to stave it off, muttering "Why Lord, why?" between immersions.

As usual in this part of Nepal, where a white face is an unrivalled novelty, I drew an inquisitive crowd of children. Usually they want to touch my lily white skin and freckles, or pull my red hair, to check whether I am real, or perhaps a Martian made out of plastic. On this occasion I was particularly fascinating because they could see almost all of me. I also used a liquid hair shampoo from England rather than a bar of soap like normal people. But the battery razor was the *tour de force*. I hope I haven't started a trend.

Shoba and Lok were very proud of the portable water filter through which they filled my life preserving water bottle from the river. I was less impressed with the thick sediment it produced, and added a purification tablet for safety. Pradeep just filled his bottle from the centre of the stream and it was crystal pure.

Thus refreshed, we set out to walk the massive Anku Khola valley towards fabled Jharlang, the Ganesh Himal and Tibet. Our quest was simply to visit the hilltop village of Bhirchet where Lok had his church, but apparently even here no white man had ever been before. I wanted to carry on to Jharlang and beyond, but I had a deadline in Kathmandu to re-confirm my airline ticket to England.

You might imagine that walking up the large valley of a major river was a steady stroll up a slight gradient. You would be wrong. The river bed being full of monsoon water making its urgent way from the roof of the world to Calcutta's unimaginably distant Hoogly River, we used a thin path meandering up and down along the precipitous valley side, with periodic jungle excursions to get over side streams. Every so often, we crossed a landslide with barely a foothold to cling to and where one false step would send the walker crashing a hundred feet into the murderous torrent below.

By now, Pradeep's new migraine was thriving and I was seriously dehydrated. Eventually, we stumbled into the steep riverside hamlet of Ringne and stopped for lunch. We had been walking for seven hours. Lok and Shoba tucked into giant *dhal bhat*, with seconds and thirds of rice, vegetables and lentil soup. Pradeep ate three peanuts and collapsed in a dark corner, muttering, 'Why, Lord, why?' He is the only walker I know who needs to walk at night and sleep in the day.

The proprietress was fat and jolly. 'Jolly' was normal round here, but 'fat' was decidedly rare. I asked her if she had anything to drink apart from dirty river water. "Mango Fruity cartons", she said, and I nearly hugged her, but my arms would not have been long enough. When I had drunk seven straight cartons of this nectar, I found I finally had enough saliva in my mouth to chew and swallow one biscuit. I told the fat lady, "You are my Fruity Queen forever."

The Fruity Queen had recently been on a diet and cut her weight from 86 kilos to 80, though there was still plenty hanging out of the 'sari gap'. She was also extremely cross with her husband and wished the whole world to know the reason why. So I am quite sure she would not mind me repeating this. He had lost their six goats in the jungle through which we were about to walk. What Pradeep thoughtfully failed to add in his translation at the time was that it seemed they had been eaten by the leopards.

Getting bored, Lok had a wander through the village while Pradeep had his snooze. He came across a man hobbling with a swollen and septic ankle in the doorway of his house. He had been in pain with it for thirteen months, becoming increasingly incapacitated. Lok explained that the hospital in Tansen could cure the ankle if he could get there. He wrote the instructions down and signed the paper so the hospital would know Lok had sent the man. But he had no money for the trip. He would have to borrow from the moneylender at a huge rate of interest and he might be in debt for life. Lok and I drew aside and I slipped him the needed 500 rupee note (£5). Lok sternly told the man he would be back this way again. So if the man hadn't spent the money getting to the hospital at Tansen, he would demand twice as much back as he had given. The man and his wife seemed grateful, and determined to give the hospital a try. The man and his wife were Hindus, but that didn't stop Lok helping. Sometimes he would pray, sometimes he would send to hospitals, but usually he seemed to do something about human need.

As we set off, perhaps to take his mind off the leopards, Lok was being encouraging. "It's only four hours more up the valley and then we just have to climb that hill," he said, pointing impossibly high in the sky. 'That hill' was the size of Snowdon on top of Ben Nevis, seven miles of walking from bottom to top. "And it's a good hill for leeches—they never attack your feet and legs like on other hills." That's a relief, I thought, knowing the humidity had reduced my matches for burning off leeches to a wet pulp. "No! On that hill it's the type that climb trees and drop on your head as you pass underneath," he grinned.

I plodded on, wondering how badly I wanted to be the first white man in Bhirchet. I saw mirages of Bavarians in Lederhosen holding out Biersteins. But, fortunately, Pradeep was in a worse state than me and kept collapsing in the shade or throwing up behind a rock. Lok was being patient and smiling, but Pradeep's pace clearly wasn't suiting him. Lok spent much of his time charging about the country on behalf of the NCF. Sometimes it was on buses, sometimes on foot. On foot he was a hard man to keep up with, and Pradeep couldn't.

As the valley bottom broadened to a white rock and sand flood plain, we descended to it and walked up the baking valley floor.

Two Christian ladies known to Lok overtook us and fell into conversation. It seemed the older one, Chhaldi Tamang, was a leader in the very church we were aiming for. In Nepali caste Hindu society, women were usually very shy, and were hardly ever leaders. Equality was a foreign concept. But the Tamang women had always been strong and forceful, like The Fruity Queen. Chhaldi exuded confidence, initiative and motherly concern. It was no wonder at all that she had emerged as a church leader.

Eventually, Lok was persuaded to take Pradeep's migraine seriously, and we all laid hands and prayed as Pradeep slumped by the river bank, clutching his umbrella, feebly trying to cool himself with the water, and mumbling, "Why, Lord, why?" The Lord still did not reply, though he did later. Chhaldi, oblivious no doubt to the fact that her nose ring was now fashionable in the West, soothed his head with her hands and anointed him with some sort of exotic Himalayan unguent, doubtless gathered from jungle herbs as yet unknown to science. Pradeep seemed to respond to the mothering, but still failed to muster enthusiasm for climbing that hill.

Shoba decided the only thing to do was to carry Pradeep himself. Chhaldi took his rucksack and a half, Shoba adjusted his headband to carry the weight, and Lok hoisted Pradeep aboard. It was a gallant effort, but doomed to failure because Pradeep was considerably bigger and heavier than Shoba. After a few staggers, a couple of photos and much laughter, Shoba dumped his load in defeat. Pradeep would have to continue under his own steam, getting crosser and crosser with the Lord who failed to take away his 'thorn in the flesh', this migraine that was spoiling the expedition for everybody. The "Why, Lord, why?" was getting more and more exasperated with the all-powerful master of men and migraines.

Lok mentioned casually as we walked further up the riverbed, the great hill of Bhirchet looming closer, that, when I got to the top, he would call the faithful together and I could preach The Word to my heart's content. I sat down on a rock to try and take in this exciting news, but the rock burnt my legs. I stood up and took a swig from my water bottle to gain time for thought, but it scalded my tongue.

Now was the time to act. Pradeep had just thrown up again, and I made a decisive, statesmanlike speech, which Pradeep had to interpret in a feeble whisper. "This man is in no condition to climb that hill." I pointed vertically into the sky. "We will have to find him lodgings in that distant village at the bottom of it. As he is my interpreter, there is no point in me climbing the hill without him, as my sermon, brilliant though it may be, will be wasted on people who only speak Tamang. I must stay with him and nurse him back to health. You, Lok Bahadur, can climb the hill and bring your people to the bottom of it in the cool of the morning. There I will interview them for my book and preach a fine sermon by the river."

I knew that Lok Bahadur would have to capitulate. At least he would now be able to trot up the hill unencumbered by a Bible teacher from Pokhara with a migraine and a vicar from England who had carried a full rucksack for twelve hours up and down mountains in a sauna and lost half his body weight in sweat.

My heart leapt at Lok's reply. The depth of self-sacrificial Christian maturity in his reply convinced me I was writing about the right man. Suppressing his obvious eagerness to sprint up the hill rejoicing, to minister to his flock, Lok said that he personally had no need to go to the village on this occasion. Anyway, it was his duty to stay with us. Instead, these two ladies will walk briskly up the hill in the cool of the dusk, and alert the elders of the church who will descend in the morning to meet us at the bottom.

The ladies smiled at us, a little knowingly I thought. A few minutes later, as we carried on walking, two elderly men breezed past us, holding ton weight *dokos* on their head bands. Spotting us, they slowed down and started chatting. They also were Christians and were going, lo and behold, up the hill to Bhirchet. Chhaldi chatted them up for a while, and then explained to me that she had a very dramatic

Christian testimony the Lord wished me to hear. It was her duty to stay with the sick man until I could interview her in the morning. These two old codgers will be the ones gleefully to sprint up the hill with the exciting summons to the elders to descend, meet their senior pastor and hear the great preacher from England, in translation by Pradeep the Migraine.

There is, as they say, one, or in this case, two, born every minute. The two grizzled veterans bounded off, thrilled to be entrusted with such a vital message by Christian leaders all selflessly sacrificing their own pilgrimage up the hill to minister to our poor, dear brother, Pradeep.

And so we reached the lodgings at the foot of the hill. The rice stood tall in the gentle terraces on the flat, hot land by a bend in the Anku Khola, and a whole house was shown off proudly to us. "Plenty of room," said Shoba, "what a pity there is only one bed between six of us."

Eventually, *dhal bhat* began to cook, and more beds arrived. Then Pradeep turned up—in the end we had left him to fend for himself on the river bed and he crawled in more dead than alive. As he collapsed on my bed, on the grounds it was in the darkest corner, I said, "Praise the Lord, brother, today you have saved six people from that flippin' hill!"

"By the way," I asked as his eyes began to close. "What was that exotic ointment Chhaldi anointed you with?" "Vic's Vapours," replied Pradeep, full of respect.

Over supper, the others chatted in Nepali while they ate their *dhal bhat* and I looked at mine. By now, in the dark, the headache had gone and nocturnal Pradeep was being the life and soul of the party. As they talked and laughed away, I asked him what they were all saying. "Well," said

Pradeep, "Shoba was saying how sore his ankle is. He crocked it in Jomson last week, and two other porters had to carry him for five days to get to the road. But his arm hurts even more than his ankle. And Lok Bahadur is saying, "Oh, my legs ache. I don't think I can make it up those steep steps to bed tonight. And how are you feeling?" Pradeep concluded, concerned. "Fine, actually," I replied in wonderment.

CHAPTER 22

THE ELDERS DESCEND

At eight next morning, five leaders from the church arrived from Bhirchet. Four had, literally, run down the hill for two hours. This meant it would have taken us six hours to plod up it. The fifth, Khari Bahadur, turned up by chance with his team of ten mules, the heavy goods vehicles of the hills. As Khari had to get to Dhading Town that night to load his mules, we interviewed him first.

"We used to worship all sorts of gods, we had the lot in our house! I had twelve buffalo and all of them died, and I thought it must be because the gods are angry with me. At the same time, our cow was pregnant and it miscarried. And then my wife miscarried our third child. It was 1988. I thought to myself, 'If these gods exist they are just destroying us, so we should give them up and go with these new Christians instead.' I got baptised by Lok Bahadur and I gave some land on which to build the church. It was such a relief to be out of all those religious ceremonies that do no good. Now I have Jesus, who feels like a father to me. I feel guided and protected by Him.

"When we became Christians, my brother-in-law and a gang of other relatives came and started destroying our house—the front of it was all broken and smashed up. They were really looking for me, but found my wife and beat her up badly. I had been able to run away and hide, otherwise they might have killed me. That evening, one of the village leaders, Kundung Lama, came and told my brother-in-law and his crowd not to attack the Christians any more. He must have seen some good in us because, though he wasn't a Christian then, he is now! That's how we were saved.

"I've mortgaged my land with the Agricultural Bank and bought the mules with the money. As well as making a living with them, it means I can transport anything the church needs for free, and I get around the whole area keeping the Christians in touch. Now I'm known as 'The old man who tithes a lot'—I've got very experienced at tithing and that's one reason why the church runs so well. But I'm doing okay with the mules—Jesus looks after us when we keep faith with Him."

"We waved Khari and his beautifully cared-for mules on their way. They looked as good as the donkeys on Scarborough beach, an eloquent testimony to the consideration of a Christian businessman.

"Where shall we go for the rest of the interviews?" I asked. We were upstairs in the house, under the dark eaves, and hidden from view. But it was pretty dark and dingy and it looked a lovely morning outside. "Much more prudent to stay upstairs in private," said Lok. You stay there talking while I go off and see a few people." So, the pastor disappeared for a while as Pradeep and I talked to Lem

Bahadur, who had just run down the hill with the other elders.

"It was eight years ago. Our daughter and then our son both died within a month of being born. My mother and my wife were both very ill as well. My wife said, 'We've exhausted all the Buddhist rituals and they've done us no good. Maybe, if we believe in Jesus we'll get better. Sun Bahadur next door is a Christian now, I think I'll go round and ask him about it.' So she went round several times, and Sun talked to her and she told me when she got home. After about six months, she took me round to his house and he gave me a booklet called, 'A way to live'. It talked about the beauty of the world and how it was made by a Creator God who loves us. It changed my life. I gave up all the Buddhist practices and became a Christian. Then we had another son, Pradip, and he's now seven years old. He was the first child dedicated in the church at Bhirchet, the first child in the village to be brought up as a Christian from the moment of his birth. Now everyone celebrates his birthday as a sort of birthday for the church."

"So", I queried, "you became a Christian not because you found that God healed you, but because you realised that, through the beauty of creation and the gift of Jesus, God the Father loved you?" "Yes, that's true but then my wife and mother both got better, and God gave us a healthy son!

"Then six years ago we had trouble. There were only three or four houses in the village with committed Christians, and so we were easy to pick on. The Village Development Committee called and said they had passed a local law—if I wanted to stay a Christian I would have to pay a fine of 10,000 Rupees. I refused to pay it, so one day a large gang appeared in our front yard. We had a fairly prosperous shop, but they looted it and took all the stock. Then they broke our nice slate roof and smashed all our doors. Some of them waited in the yard with flaming torches to set fire to the house. They were hoping to catch us inside. But we had managed to slip away. For a whole year we were never able to eat or drink or sleep at home, though we slipped in occasionally. The whole family, including the baby, lived in caves and out in the jungle with only water to drink. We did a lot of praying that year.

"Eventually, the Village Chairman told me they had passed another law; now no one would associate with the Christians. We were to be separated out and excluded from all the village events and society. We had to choose whether to belong to our society or to belong to Jesus. Some believers gave in and said they would give up Jesus. But ten of us said we would give up their society. The ten of us began meeting in our house, and the total offering at our first service was 4.5 rupees! After a year, we had to move to somewhere bigger, and two years ago we built a proper church on Khari's land. We thought it was huge at the time, but it's too small already. The offering now averages about 135 rupees."

"You're not the church treasurer are you, by any chance?" I asked. "I used to be, but not now. You'll meet the new treasurer later," he replied. Pradeep put his finger to his lips and pointed outside. I looked down, and there was the local witch doctor, his hair plaited and curled round his back, snooping around, looking through the door, trying to find out what was going on. Suddenly, there was a whiff of fear in the air, a tangible reminder of the life and death power struggle that was being waged in these hills between the old and the new.

"What do you think about living in Bhirchet?" I asked, when the witch doctor moved on. "Oh, everybody moves away if they can afford it. They try to earn money abroad—my younger brother's in Malaysia at the moment. Then, when they have some money, they buy land on the Terai and move there. Well, it's no fun living on top of that hill. Wouldn't you move somewhere flat if you could? But I won't move, because it's the church that's important to me. It's really growing now. We've got a Youth Fellowship, Home Groups and a Prayer Meeting.""How did you find out about things like that?" I asked, thinking about Bhirchet's almost impenetrable isolation. "We started them because the antique man told us to," came the answer. "Antique man?" I queried. "Yes, the antique pastor!" he grinned. "Ah, Lok Bahadur, the fifty-two year old antique!" I smiled. They were all obviously very fond of him, but for a young church no more than about eight years old, a man who had been a believer for forty years was clearly a Christian Methuselah.

The team had got themselves well organised and, as we said our thanks to Lem, Nar Bahadur slipped into his seat for his interview. Like Lem, he farmed his land in Bhirchet, and he had three children. He was short, even by Nepali standards, with a faded check shirt and shorts that had seen better days.

"When I was a boy, my father was very sick. We had the witch doctor in to cast out evil spirits with spells, but nothing worked and he never got better. Then one night a group of travellers lodged with us overnight. They turned out to be Christians and they prayed with my father and gave him a copy of the Gospels as a present. The next morning, he started getting better. He read the Gospels and kept them but he didn't do anything about them. I never forgot what the Christians did, but when a small church started in Bhirchet I was too scared of what other people would say to join in.

"Then I went away and got a good job in India. I was earning a lot of money, but about four years ago I got sick with stomach ulcers so I came home for a while. I felt ill physically, but I realised I also felt restless and ill at ease emotionally. I had no peace. So I picked up the old copy of the Gospels those people had given my father and I read them. Simply reading the Gospels made me want to be a Christian, and suddenly I felt a wonderful peace come over me. I realised that my life's purpose was to honour God, not earn money, so I resigned my job. And then God healed my stomach as well.

"A little later, Lok Bahadur sent me on a five-month Pastoral Training Course. I got a great blessing from the course and God spoke to me in lots of different ways. I discovered for the first time just how much God loved me. I also realised that, although I knew the Gospel with my mind, I was behaving as though I didn't know it at all. I learnt how to live as a good Christian in my family and personal life, and in the church. Love for others—that's the heart of it! Now I've decided to stay in Bhirchet and serve the Lord here, I'm happy and fulfilled—I preach, counsel those in trouble, and help to pastor the people."

I thanked Lem and wished him well. Pradeep was still on top of things, sheltered as he was in the darkness of the eaves of the house wearing his sunglasses. So we were able to carry straight on.

Chhaldi looked quite refreshed after her night at the bottom of the hill, and eager to talk. I asked her where she was coming back from with the other lady when they caught us up. "She's got epilepsy," said Chhaldi, "and she spent some time in India where it got much worse. I took her to a church in Dhading Town to be prayed for, but I don't think she's been healed yet". Chhaldi seemed confident it would only be a matter of time.

"I used to suffer from migraine headaches, so I know what Pradeep feels like. I went to thirteen different Buddhist monks and witch doctors and all of them tried to cure me—casting out evil spirits and that sort of thing. But nothing worked. Then in 1989 I met a young lad of twenty who had epilepsy. Some Christians prayed for him and he was healed. He told me that God could heal me too. So one night, secretly, I went out to find him and he prayed for me. I felt I was getting better, so I went back to him several times, and each time he prayed for me I got better still. So I began to believe in Jesus secretly but I was too scared to be open about it until 1991.

"When I had the courage to go public and meet with the other Christians, people all said it was a stupid, low caste thing to do and I should give it up while I had the chance. Then one day I was praying with my two nephews, who had also become Christians. A group of people caught us praying and tied our hands together in *doko* ropes. We were all handcuffed and roped together like animals. Then the men in the gang started punching us, and the women kicked me on the back. But I wasn't going to give up because I was beaten up. Then my elder brother got drunk one night. His friends egged him on and he came round and beat me up for being a Christian. I've prayed for him and his wife ever since. His wife is a Christian now, but he isn't yet.

"The next day, the neighbours all came round. 'Listen lady,' they said, 'even your own brother beats you up, so give up your religion now.' I told them, 'I will give up my own brother, but I will not give up my Lord Jesus.' Then the most important lady in the village came round to try and persuade me. I told her the same thing—'No, I'll give up the whole world but I'll follow Christ.' I was so firm about it, I've had no hassle since. I think they just gave up on me. But other Christians who were more frightened, and who perhaps gave in to pressure once, are much more persecuted now than I am."

Chhaldi was full of charisma, vitality and joy, with a large laugh and a wonderful line in mothering—a natural leader. This was unusual and frowned upon in Caste Hindu society, but the Tamang Christian women were liberated from the old repression.

"What else can you tell me about yourself, Chhaldi?" I asked. "I'm very sorry," she apologised, "Since I've become a Christian, I don't have much to say about myself. Jesus has taken all my worries and burdens away. I'm not really interested in myself anymore. The interesting thing now is the help and prayer I offer to others."

"Well, I'm excited to meet a Christian who is more interested in other people's problems than their own!" I responded, "We could do with a few more like you."

CHAPTER 23

THE PASTOR WITH A PRICE ON HIS HEAD

Just occasionally it is possible to meet a Tamang whose middle name is not 'Bahadur'. In came the young pastor of Bhirchet, and he wrote in my notebook, in English, 'My name is Uddab Sing Tamang.'

"I'm from Kuri, just down the valley from here. We were a very strong Buddhist family. My father and grandfather were monks and witch doctors, and I began to do the same things. These old witch doctors could do quite powerful things—they could walk on fire and they could levitate. On the surface, they used their knowledge for good—casting out evil spirits and ghosts and things like that. But for money, secretly, they would do evil things like put a curse on someone to kill them. I learned all the magic spells and incantations necessary to be a witch doctor, but I just didn't get enough custom to make a living at it. So I became a

Buddhist monk for a while and wore the red cloth. I went to the monastery and learnt their ways of healing.

"Then my third sister came to Kuri on a visit. She lived in Kanchanpur, four days walk to the west, and she was a Christian. She took me through the Bible from Genesis to Revelation. She told me about creation and sin and judgement, and about the life of Jesus. 'You shouldn't hang on to these occult things—they're dangerous', she told me. Then a group of six people came to Kuri from Kathmandu, distributing booklets. I read one of them and I believed that Jesus was real, and felt that his Holy Spirit was working inside me. So I became a Christian. I wasn't like many of the others who became Christians because they were healed. I became a Christian because I realised it was true. Jesus was real! That was in 1989.

"At first, I believed the good news but I didn't live it. I carried on drinking and fighting a lot, and I used to steal chickens and pigs and go to another village to sell them. Then I got beaten up. I think God allowed it to happen because I wasn't living as a Christian should, so I blame myself. A crowd of about seventy people converged on me and started hitting me because I was a Christian. They got me to the ground, some of them kicked my head and others stood on my chest. They were trying to finish me off. As this was happening, I prayed to the Lord, "If you have any use for me in my life, let me live through this." When I'd prayed, one of my attackers shouted, 'Now let's take this chap to his sister's'. So they carted me off and dumped me at my second sister's house. They left me there for dead. My skull was fractured and my scalp was separated from my head. My head's still deformed today. My digestive system was destroyed and everything ended up in my trousers. Afterwards, I could digest no food whatsoever. I'd just survived the attack but I was dying anyway.

"But my sister had just had a baby, and she started giving me her own milk to drink. I found I could digest that, and so I survived, on my sister's milk. The gang all thought I was dying, but the Lord gave me a new life. That's when the word went round the village—'Jesus was killed and came back to life. Now it's happened to Uddab. So this time, let's do it properly. Let's get the Kukhuris out and slice him in two halves!' At that time, all the local Christians were scattered and in hiding. So as soon as I was strong enough, I escaped and went down to Barataidi to find Lok Bahadur. He was the most well known Christian leader and he would help me.

"I found out that everybody had heard about me, and there were Christians in Butwal, Pokhara, Tansen, Barataidi and Bhirchet, who were praying that I would survive. So, it's no wonder I did!

"I stayed with Lok Bahadur for a while, and he sent me to a training centre for three months. So I gained strength both physically and spiritually. Eventually, he sent me back to join the Christians at Bhirchet and help start the church. The numbers of believers quickly increased after I arrived, but so did the persecution. A local Lama was a very wealthy man, and he offered a reward of 60,000 rupees to anyone who brought him my severed head. He also guaranteed to lay out 200,000 rupees to spring the murderer out of jail if necessary. So I had a price on my head of 260,000 rupees (about £2500)!

"It was monsoon time and, of course, I was hiding out in the caves and trees, praying and fasting and thinking. Eventually, I decided I needed more knowledge before I could do the job in Bhirchet properly, so I slipped away and went to Bible College in India for two years. When I got back, in 1992, there were thirty-five members of the church, and now, after five years, there are 275. We've also started fifteen daughter churches, so it all adds up to at least 1000! I'm particularly thankful that at least seven out of that crowd of seventy are Christians now. Even the Lama isn't against me any more, though we're still in the minority here and it's still dangerous.

"I'm not sure what will happen in the future. Three times now, I've had a vision. Angels arrive with a letter for me that says I'm about to die and go to heaven. It's a sort of summons from God. In the vision I say to the angels, 'These people need me here, I can't leave yet. Please let me stay.' And then the angels take their letter away. But one day, I expect it will get delivered properly."

CHAPTER 24

LOVE CONQUERS ALL

A second lady prayer warrior had come down the mountain with the other elders. Her name was Thum Bhajum. She seemed to spend her life up on Bhirchet hill, and knew little Nepali. We needed two translators some of the time—one from Tamang into Nepali, then Pradeep into English. "So where," I agonised, "Did she get her 'United Colours of Benetton' sweatshirt from?"

"I gather you're the new church treasurer," I essayed. "Yes, I know nothing but I'm the treasurer!" she laughed. "Pradeep," I said, "I don't think she can read and write, can she add up?" Pradeep decided to give Thum Bhajum a test. "If you had 20 rupees and someone gave you 50 paise (half a rupee), how much would you have?" Thum responded gleefully, "I haven't a clue, only the Lord knows things like that!"

So, I had found a church treasurer who really couldn't add up, and admitted it! But Thum had a more important quality than numeracy—apart from being full of life and fun she was honest and trustworthy. She took the church collection, put it into her box, and removed it when the elders needed to spend money. As long as there was still some money in the box, the church was solvent. So there were no accounts, no auditors and no church council meetings worrying about how little was in the bank account. It was all wonderfully simple. I liked it.

Then I asked Thum how long she had been a Christian.

"Since 1990. I was tired of the old occult rituals. They made me miserable and gave me odd and disturbing thoughts. My eldest son, Ambra Bahader, also became a Christian. He was a young schoolteacher in the village and his wife had just had their first child. Ambra was a quiet Christian and he didn't try to convert others. But he did have a Bible, and one day he was caught reading it. A gang beat him up, just because he was reading his Bible, and, when he was on the floor, they kicked him repeatedly on the chin. He lingered for a while, but finally he died of internal bleeding.

"After that, I was followed and checked up on, especially if I met other Christians. Then my husband died, and they put pressure on me to marry a good Buddhist. It was hard to bring up the younger children by myself with no husband's income, but I was determined to stay a Christian. Whatever happened, I was still going to love Jesus. So now I'm a church caretaker, the treasurer, and I spend a lot of time praying for people."

"What do you think about the people who killed your son?" I asked her, quietly.

"I know who the killers are—they're all neighbours. At the time, though, I couldn't say anything because the village authorities were on their side. If I had made a fuss they might well have killed me. Now, I have a great love for them because Jesus said, "Love your enemies, bless those who persecute you," and I love to obey Jesus. That gives me great joy. After all, we beat up and killed God's Son, and He forgives us, so I must forgive as well. Some of them have since become Christians, so now they are my brothers."

Thum Bhjum's story triggered a picture of Golgotha in my mind. From the cross, Jesus said, "Father forgive them for they know not what they do." But what about his mother? Was Mary able to forgive the killers of her son? We are not told. But Thum Bhajum's extraordinary forgiveness, courage, love, strength and humour gave me hope that Mary could have forgiven even those who pierced her own soul when they crucified her son. And, if so, she would have known healing of mind and spirit within the body of the first Christian Church.

"I never thought of giving up being a Christian," Thum went on, "I'll always remain a Christian even if our enemies cut me in pieces. When these things happen, I'm more jealous for the Lord and trust Him more. I'm not young but I'm now learning to read so I can study my Bible and learn more."

Thum Bhajum was just one of many Nepalis whose motive for becoming literate was to read their own Bible. But there was a special courage in her case. She was learning to do what her neighbours had already killed her son for doing.

"But prayer is my greatest joy. Three months ago, some of the Christian men in the church went to a nearby village to share the Gospel. The villagers surrounded them and looked liked they were going to beat them up. But we ladies had stayed behind and were praying together continuously for their safety. That's why they were saved from the beating. Now I pray all the time if I can. It's a wonderful, joyous thing, and there is enormous power in prayer."

So it was I realised that Thum Bhajum had learnt as well as any of her people that, in Christ, and by the grace of God, joy conquers pain, prayer conquers evil, forgiveness conquers sin, faith conquers fear, zeal conquers unbelief, courage conquers the world, and love conquers all. To her faith and witness I heard the angels cry 'Amen' and 'Amen' and 'Amen'.

CHAPTER 25

A LANDSLIDE TO THE CHRISTIANS

When the landslide ended Lok's childhood, there were no Christians in Dhading District. When Lok returned to find a wife, he was the first Christian in his area. Even ten years ago when I first walked in these hills, on the Gorkha side, there were hardly any Christians. The friendly greeting between travellers was the universal Hindu 'Namaste' (I salute the God within you). But, as we set out from Dhading Town on this trip, a surprising number of porters and travellers sized us up, recognised Lok Bahadur, realised we were Christians, broke out into huge grins, joyfully put their hands together as for prayer, and proudly greeted us with "Jai Masih" (Hail to the Messiah). In the last few years it seemed the Christians had multiplied beyond counting.

As we got further into these remote hills it was clear there were more and more of them. Christians were becoming as thick on the ground as priests at a papal mass. And they were obviously overjoyed with their new religion, free at last from fear of their mountain gods and from their expensive witch doctors. Now they had a God much higher than any mountain, who poured out love and free grace from His high throne. He answered their prayers and offered them hope. No foreign missionaries had trod these paths, just Lok Bahadur and a few other pioneers among the Tamang people. The power of God and the courage of Christians seem to have grown the church. It was now all much bigger than one man. It was a mass movement out of the control of any one person, movement or Government. This potent mix of the power of God and the courage of man seemed to be unstoppable.

"We Tamangs," explained Lok, "have always been a wild, violent, unruly bunch. Quite a lot were no more than bandits. It's no wonder they made good Gurkhas for the British army. Even the military here couldn't control them. The Dhading hills are too tough and rough even for the Nepalese Army, let alone anyone else's. Eventually, the king built a gate and a wall at Jharlang and said, 'I'll try to control everything to the south of the wall and I'm leaving everything to the north of the wall to the uncontrollable Tamangs.' But even the toughest, most violent of them still lived their lives in fear of the gods like my village did." Lok pointed to the giant hill a few miles up the Anku Khola Valley where the landslide in 1955 had changed his life for ever. Jesus the redeemer had certainly transformed that disaster into His triumph.

"But now the whole culture is changing because the people change when they become Christians. They stop their drunkenness and their wild mountain ways. They become more content, gentle, joyful. They love each other instead of fighting. They work harder and more effectively so they get more prosperous. They get themselves educated and learn to read. The old fears and violence are going. Even the fear of unofficial persecution is finished now in the areas where the Christians are a majority and running the *panchayats*. Lots of the *lamas* and *bombos* (witch doctors) have become Christians themselves. One day soon we hope that the whole of Nepal will be like this. In the country as a whole only one or two per cent are Christians, but we are hoping for ten percent within five years. Of course, out here it's much more than that already."

A landslide to the Christians.

"In the meantime, we have to be careful in areas like Bhirchet where the Christians are still in a minority. We're winning the war but there are plenty of battles to fight yet."

Lunch was served by Shoba. Piles of *dhal bhat*, Himlayan high, were demolished by the others and re-arranged by me. "We are very disappointed with you," they teased me, "for not climbing our beautiful hill and preaching in our new church at the top. You must promise us you will come again when you have more time or we'll put extra *dhal bhat* on your plate.""Okay," I said, "But it will have to be in winter when it's less humid!" The promise safely elicited, Uddab then remarked, "By the way, it is perhaps as well you didn't come to the village last night after all. You may have heard that a very important Buddhist in the village was very sick.""Oh yes, travellers coming the other way kept mentioning it while we walked."

"Yes, he died yesterday. Last night, all the Buddhist men were in a gang near the church getting drunk at the funeral. They were working up into a real frenzy. If you had arrived in the middle of it with the church leaders they would have thought you were the source of all this new Christianity and killed you!"

I found my reaction to this startling news quite surprising. I burst out laughing and turned to Pradeep. "Now you've got your answer to 'Why Lord, why?' It was the Lord's migraine, Pradeep. It didn't just save us from climbing that flippin' hill, it saved me from being a martyr. You have a very unusual ministry!"

Lok Bahadur seemed to be saying similar things in Nepali and quoting Romans 8:28. Out in Dhading this sort of danger and escape were still common enough and it was an honour to be part of it. Now I understood my premonition of danger and was confident at last of returning in one piece to my German speaking canine friend in Kathmandu. Being the first Vicar of Scarborough to be martyred had never really appealed to me. Most of all, it was wonderful fun being a Christian on the roof of the world, sharing joy and jokes with those who had come through the fires of persecution sustained by the God with a great sense of humour. However, I did make a mental note to delay my return to Bhirchet for a few years until Uddab and his friends had finished the job and converted the whole area.

After marvelling at the sovereignty of God and promising Pradeep a bonus for being the hero of the hour, I then settled down to listen to a special request from Uddab.

"In the last eight years, since the church at Bhirchet began, no Christian has died of natural causes. With the daughter churches there are a thousand of us by now, of all ages. Life expectancy round here is pretty low. On average in eight years perhaps one in seven of us would normally die. So not a single one out of a thousand is quite unusual. What we do is this. Whenever a Christian is seriously ill, prayer warriors from the church gather round, fast and pray for them, in relays if necessary. Chhaldi and Thum Bhajum are two of them. They'll keep this up continuously for days if they have to. If a Christian were to die, the Buddhists would all say, 'See, your Christian God has gone to sleep, he'll be no more use to you any more.' So we pray our people back to health to prevent the name of Jesus being ridiculed and to encourage the Buddhists to become Christians themselves. This is the main reason why our church is growing so fast. So far, nobody has died and everybody has got better."

The elders nodded their heads in agreement. "It even works with the animals," they added. "If the animals die, we might starve to death as well. Even the dogs get better." I had a sudden vision of twenty year old dogs staggering about at the top of the hill, unable to reach the great kennel in the sky because their owners kept praying them back to life. "Are you telling me," I asked, "That no dog belonging to a Christian has ever died in eight years?"

"No, none," said some of them. "Oh yes they have, what about So and So's dog," retorted others. "But So and So wasn't a Christian at the time." Forgetting me for a while, they had a fine argument about the dogs, though they were unanimous about the people and the buffalo.

"But we do realise," concluded Uddab, "That this probably can't go on for ever." I treasured the word 'Probably'.

"So we need to buy some land for a secure Christian graveyard where the *lamas* can't get at us. Everyone round here is supposed to be cremated by the *lamas* and we can't allow that to happen to the Christians. We need to give them a proper Christian burial and for that we need land. In our culture this is the big battle we have to fight. Could you buy some land for us? It would cost about 30,000 Rupees (£300)."

I was quite sure that, if my church in Scarborough bought them the land, it would bring this phase in the history of Bhirchet to an end. These amazing, isolated new Christians whose courage, faith and zeal overwhelmed and inspired me, would start dying like the rest of us.

What was I to do? It was a big responsibility. I thought deeply.

"My friends, so far you have discovered the power of Jesus. You have shown the love of God which is higher even than your great hill. You should be an inspiration to believers all over the world. You are populating the Himalayas with Christians and transforming a whole people. But there is somewhere even greater and more beautiful than Dhading to populate—a mountain higher than Everest to climb. Soon you must witness not only to the power of Jesus to heal, but also to the power of Jesus to raise you to eternal life. You have been tested by illness, soon you must be tested by bereavement. So far you offer the hope of healing, now you must hold out the hope of Heaven. You must populate not just the hills of Dhading but Heaven itself. Jesus has already bought your victory over the grave but I think my church will buy your graveyard."

And so it did. One day I shall return to climb the big hill of Bhirchet, to rejoice with these courageous Christians converted from fear to faith, to share again the love of God which is higher than the hills, and to pray by the mountain-top graves of those who have conquered death itself to populate the highest hills of Heaven.

TILL THE FAT LADY SINGS

BOB JACKSON

An outrageous mixture of

Barchester and Ambridge!

St Agatha's is a welcoming, middle-of-the-road parish church in the centre of a town called Yawtown. The Revd Vincent Popplethwaite is a pretty unassuming sort of a vicar – he only wishes that everyone would stop considering clergy as a breed apart.

Bob Jackson has written a brilliantly satirical, at times risqué and yet affectionate novel which tells how the good people of St Agatha's confront and come to terms with some of the greater (and lesser) issues which insistently lap at the shores of today's church.

Meanwhile, beyond human agencies, there are signs that the Holy Spirit is accelerating his work – not to mention the Grim Reaper.

ISBN 1 897913 29 X

Highland Books   Price £4.99

Shut Up Sarah

Marion Field

Was she privileged? Sarah was born into the Taylorites, the most exclusive of those Brethren who look to J N Darby as founder. You may have seen them:

- Women with scarves who stick together
- Schoolchildren who never accept invitations
- Groups of men declaiming the Bible in a shopping street

This true story of a teenage daughter refusing to be browbeaten by either family or elders will be compulsive reading for mature teenagers struggling between loyalty and the need of change—as well as for any who want to understand how certain Brethren could have lost their way.

> *'I highly recommend this book … This gifted writer in her second book has written a true story in a compelling fictional style.'*
> **Jennifer Rees-Larcombe**

ISBN 1-897913-28-1

Highland Books   Price £5.99

A Window To Heaven

Dr Diane M. Komp

W hat would you do as a hospital doctor when children facing death—or their parents—witness to you about faith? The official line is not to get involved, to stay 'professional'. But that was not Dr Komp's reaction ...

'I have met people who claim they lost their faith over the agonising question, How can a loving God let innocent children die? Dr Komp is the first person I've met who found a personal faith while treating such dying children. Her story —and theirs— deserves our attention'.
Philip Yancey
Author of *Disappointment with God*

'Unforgettably inspiring'
Sandy Millar, Holy Trinity Brompton

'Out of harrowing experiences while looking after children with cancer, Diane Komp, a paediatric oncologist of international repute, draws conclusions about the human condition that should make us pause and think ...
I read it with a lump in my throat.'
J.S. Malpas D.Phil., FRCP, FRCR, FFPM
St Bartholomew's Hospital, London
ISBN 1-897913-32-X
Highland Books   Price £3.99

THE
STRENGTH OF
A MAN
DAVID ROPER

This book is for men who are hungry for spiritual growth; it will strike a particular chord with those who find it natural to signal their masculinity either positively (all-male sports, perhaps) or by what they don't do (maybe ironing or dancing).

It contains 50 short (max. 4 pages!), sharply-observed jottings on a wide range of topics which men have always thought about — and usually prefer to keep to themselves.

The author, a former pastor, now leads a ministry which supports pastoral couples in America.

'David Roper knows and understands men. He is also well acquainted with the One whom he calls the manliest man of all'
Stuart Briscoe

'Translates God's word into everyday living'
Rod Redhead, Maranatha Ministries

ISBN 1 897913 34 6

Highland Books   Price £6.99

REBUILDING YOUR BROKEN WORLD

GORDON MACDONALD

'Broken worlds' are failures tinged with a measure of guilt. As the author says 'there are far more broken worlds out there than anyone realises or admits.' Platitudes about learning from our mistakes are not enough; we need spiritual power to answer and then to get free from the key questions: *'How could I?'* and *'Can I avoid doing it again?'*

THE BOOK THAT HELPED PRESIDENT CLINTON DEAL IN PRIVATE WITH THE LEWINSKY SCANDAL.

'One of the most significant books of all time'
George Verwer

ISBN 0 946616 49 3

Highland Books   Price £4.50

What do most people go to Nepal to see? Nature, the wealth of animal and plantlife as well as the lofty mountains. Above, is Machhapuchhare ('The Fish Tail') which towers 6993 meters above Pokhara and where, according to ancestral beliefs, live the gods who rule their lives. *Below* Elephants in Chitwan National Park, close to Barataidi, Lok's present home.

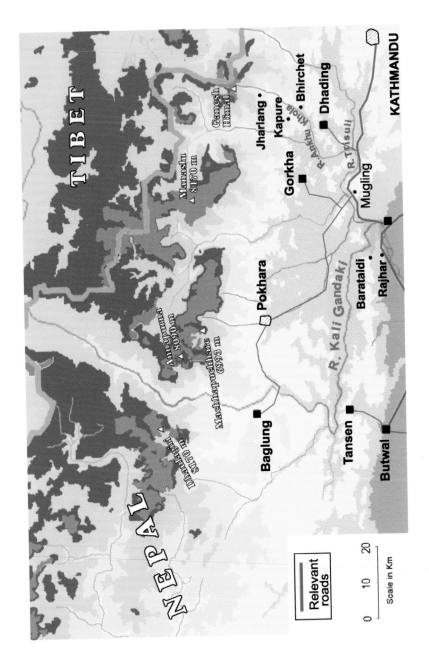

ii

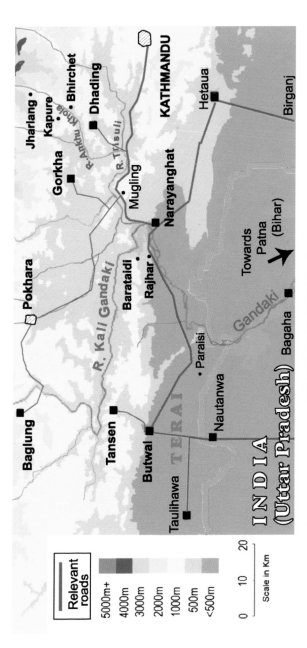

MAP OF NEPAL
with details of places mentioned

Sources for map: Microsoft Encarta, Philip's World Atlas, hand-drawn map by the author's wife, Christine

iv

Views of Barataidi, Lok's home today. Above, his courtyard complete with hen hut, pigeon loft, buffalo and goat stables—the pigeons are eaten, not raced! On the opposite page a typical home for one of Barataidi's landless poor. Below, a gathering monsoon over the village.

Three shots of Phulmaya, Lok's wife. Above, working in her kitchen; right, posing outside her home. Opposite checking out a paddy field. Inset: a butterfly seen nearby on a wild flower.

After the church meeting, a converted witch-doctor discusses the case of the disappearing Singha Bahadur, 'another Enoch' while a young, long-haired Nepali boy looks on.

Saturday church in Rajhar, women on one side and men on the other. The author has just been told he is the preacher and ushered to the front, with just the length of the Bible reading to think up his sermon and take a quick photo!

Right, Danda Lal, the church worker at Rajhar.

The disabled Dil Bahadur, who was imprisoned for his faith

Above and opposite: portraits of people who tell their story in the book (also on previous page, Danda Lal, the 'church worker').

Lem Bahadur, one of the elders of the church in Birchet (in the mountain valley where Lok was born).

Thum Bhajum, the church treasurer who can't add up, but knows the most important things!

Uddab Sing, survivor of persecutions and young pastor with a price on his head.

The 'Service Station' town of Mugling, at the junction of Terai and Pokhara roads — an island of human squalor in a sea of natural splendour. On the menu for lunch, Dhal Bhat or Snickers Bar!

Opposite page: (back row, standing) Lem, author, Lok, Nar Bahadur, Thum Bajum, Chhaldi,
(front row, squatting) Uddab and lady with epilepsy.

Right, Khari and his mules

On the way to Birchet: above, under a shade tree outside Dhading Town, Lok attracts a crowd to hear his story. Below, a bridge over a minor river on the way to Dhading. Left, trekking from Dhading to Birchet, Lok, Pradeep and Shoba. Cloud is forming in the valley below, while someone is turning up the controls of the sauna and Pradeep's migraine begins to stir.

Lok Bahadur Tamang — 'the Antique Pastor' among the hills of his birth